CONTENTS

T0089298

Introduction

Places 24

Accommodation 121

Essentials 129

TENERIFE & LA GOMERA

The islands of Tenerife and La Gomera sit side by side in the Atlantic Ocean--they're only 46km apart--but it feels like a million miles. Almost guaranteed year-round sunshine is the main reason millions of visitors flock annually to Tenerife where, in its south- and west-coast resorts, the archetypal holiday pleasures of sun, sea and sand beckon from within a safe, familiar environment. Yet outside the resorts, there's a vastly different side to Tenerife, one which more closely resembles its diminutive neighbour to the west, where ancient rainforests and ragged mountains border abyssal ravines, and at its heart sits Spain's highest mountain within a vast, volcanic crater beneath some of the world's clearest skies. At the opposite end of the tourism spectrum, La Gomera's dramatic and unspoilt landscape enjoys just a fraction of Tenerife's volume of annual visitors, many of whom travel from across Europe to hike its spectacular and demanding terrain.

Punta de Teno

Colourful balconies in Santa Cruz

Lying at the centre of the Canarian archipelago, just 186 miles off the coast of West Africa, Tenerife has been welcoming travellers since the nineteenth century when well-heeled Victorians were advised by their doctors to over-winter in the mild climate. Traditionally focusing on the budget package holiday market, the twenty-first century has seen Tenerife cast off its party island sobriquet of the 1990s with the construction of deluxe hotels along its west coast, attracting a new wave of travellers to its shores.

Away from its purpose-built resorts, Tenerife is becoming increasingly popular with those who enjoy a more active holiday. Criss-crossed by ancient trails, the island is one of Europe's finest winter walking destinations, complemented by a network of rural boutique hotels. Summer trade winds keep the island cool and create ideal conditions for sailors, surfers and windsurfers, while beneath the waves, divers find submerged basaltic columns teeming with tropical fish. In the traditional northern towns and cities that grew up around a frontier society at the crossroads of Europe and the New World, the elegant facades of colonial architecture line cobbled

When to visit

The climate across the Canary Islands is mild year-round which means there's no bad time to visit, although you're most likely to see some rain, particularly in the north, during season changes (i.e. Nov & Feb/March). High season is during the European winter, and places get especially busy from mid-December to February, when temperatures hover around 20°C. The islands are also popular at carnival (start of Lent, Feb or March), Easter and during summer holidays (June–Sept) when temperatures can get up to 30°C. September and October are particularly nice times to visit: summer temperatures still linger, but the high-season crowds haven't yet arrived.

What's new

Although impacted by the coronavirus pandemic, Tenerife's food scene has been resilient: the island has three Michelin starred restaurants, attracting a new tourism market of gastronomes. Alongside this culinary excellence, the island's wines are also enjoying a renaissance, regularly winning international awards. With 115 *bodegas* (wineries) on the island, forty of which have facilities for visitors, wine tourism looks set to blossom in the coming years. As rural tourism continues to enjoy a resurgence, particularly the hiking market, Tenerife is seeing a move towards restricting visitor numbers and charging for access. This has already happened in the Barranco del Infierno and, in 2021, Barranco de Masca reopened after being closed for three years. The new pilot programme greatly restricts the number of people that can book and enter the gorge at any one time.

streets and leafy plazas alongside bustling markets and an emergent gastronomic scene.

Lying just a forty-minute ferry ride off Tenerife's west coast, the strikingly precipitous La Gomera is a startling contrast to its populous neighbour. A lack of major beaches and resorts has preserved a sense of remoteness and left the island's laidback rural tranquillity largely to subsistence farming and trail hikers. San Sebastián, into which the ferry sails, was the final stopping off point for Columbus on his atlas-changing voyage of 1492 and provides an insight into the island's tightly knit community. The closest La Gomera gets to resorts are Valle Gran Rey in the south, which has been a hippy retreat since the 1960s, and Playa de Santiago in the west, which is dominated by the developments of the Fred Olsen family. Forming the central and highest point of the island, the ancient Garajonay rainforest pre-dates the last Ice Age, its boundaries blurring into the fertile north, where the terrain is as unforgiving as it is beautiful.

Vueltas, Valle Gran Rey

Where to...

Shop

The streets around Calle Castillo and the Meridiano and Trés de Mayo Centres provide the best clothes shopping in **Santa Cruz**, while the Sunday flea market around the African market is a good place to pick up crafty souvenirs. The best independent shops are in La Laguna, including some exciting young *tinerfeño* designers. For local produce and crafts, head to one of the islands' **farmers' markets** – try Tenerife's Teguise market (Sun 9am–2pm) or La Gomera's Valle Gran Rey Sunday market (see page 112).
OUR FAVOURITES: Pisaverde, see page 42. La Ranilla Espacio Artesano, see page 57. Casa Lercaro, see page 57.

Eat

To experience some of the island's burgeoning food scene, head to **Santa Cruz** and the Ranilla district of **Puerto de la Cruz**. There are plenty of traditional restaurants around the **north**; for a truly authentic experience, visit one of the no-frills **guachinches,** makeshift restaurants serving a few basic local dishes and wine from the owner's own harvest. Unique to Tenerife, *guachinches* have been around since the seventeenth century and can be found dotted around northern hill towns. For the best fish and seafood, head to little **San Andrés** (see page 40) alongside Playa Las Teresitas or look for the local *cofradía* (Fishermen's Guild) found in any traditional fishing town such as **Los Cristianos** or **Puerto de la Cruz**.
OUR FAVOURITES: El Rincon de Juan Carlos, see page 71. Otelo, see page 81. Casa Efigenia (La Gomera), see page 119.

Drink

Leaving the hedonistic, all-night drinking dens of the 1990s to fade into history, today's visitors to Tenerife prefer **beach lounge bars** where they can idle away an afternoon posing by an infinity pool with cocktails and chillout music; **Playa de Las Américas** and **Costa Adeje** do them particularly well. In Santa Cruz, the **Noria** district is the place to go for rooftop bars and live music while in summer, the open-air *Terraza Isla de Mar* is the venue in which to see and be seen.
OUR FAVOURITES: Mojos y Mojitos, see page 35. Kaluna, see page 82. La Casita, see page 35.

Go out

Playa de Las Américas is Tenerife's liveliest nightlife area, although the spotlight has mercifully been all but switched off for the notorious *CC Veronica's*. Nowadays it's the rows of bars around the *Parque La Paz* hotel known as "**the Patch**" that draws most visitors, with performances ranging from soul and Motown to good old rock 'n' roll. Younger crowds head to *Tramps* nightclub or *Monkey Bar* and *Papagayo* beach bar/clubs. For a more authentic taste of Tenerife's nightlife, head for **Puerto de la Cruz** and **Santa Cruz**, which cater to a local crowd after midnight at the weekend. Outside of Valle Gran Rey, nightlife on **La Gomera** is on the quiet side of laidback with few places opening beyond midnight.
OUR FAVOURITES: Blanco Bar, see page 59. Bull's Head, see page 82. Papagayo, see page 83.

Tenerife and La Gomera at a glance

Puerto de la Cruz and around p.48.
Tenerife's original resort, offering a more authentic experience and access to the best hiking. Nearby is the island's most sophisticated town, set in its eponymous fertile valley, La Orotava.

Garachico and the Teno p.60.
Lava rock pools and bags of character in the island's prettiest town, alongside the striking Teno mountains.

ATLANTIC OCEAN

TENO

Garachico

Buenavista Los Silos

Icod de los Vinos

Masca

PARQUE NACIONAL DEL TEIDE

The west coast p.68.
A string of coastal resorts running south from the foot of the giant cliffs of Los Gigantes.

Los Gigantes
Puerto Santiago
Playa de la Arena
Alcalá
Playa de San Juan

Arguayo

Chío

Guía de Isora

The southwest resorts p.72.
The holiday centre of the island, with beaches, nightlife, hotels and a 10km promenade.

Vilaflor

La Gomera
(see inset below)

Adeje

Arona

Costa Adeje
Playa de las Américas
Los Cristianos

Valle Gran Rey p.108.
Good restaurants, beaches and a hippy vibe in La Gomera's largest resort.

Las Galletas Costa Silenc

Vallehermoso

Agulo

Hermigua

El Cedro

PARQUE NACIONAL DE GARAJONAY

Arure

La Laja

San Sebastián

Valle Gran Rey

La Gomera

Alajero

ATLANTIC OCEAN

Playa de Santiago

| 0 | kilometres | 5 |
| 0 | miles | 3 |

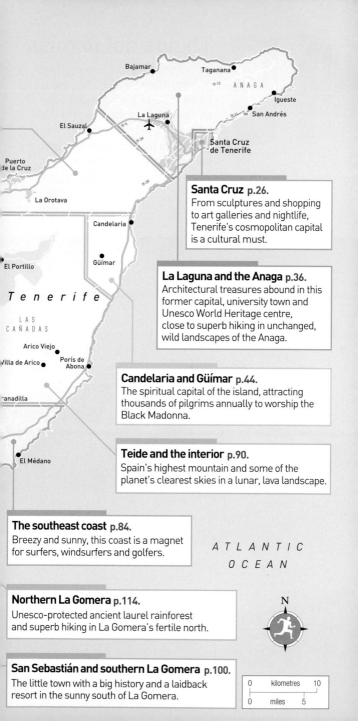

Bajamar

Taganana

ANAGA

TF-12

Igueste

TF-11

San Andrés

La Laguna

TF-5

El Sauzal

TF-24

Santa Cruz
de Tenerife

Puerto
de la Cruz

TF-28

La Orotava

Candelaria

El Portillo

Güímar

Tenerife

LAS
CAÑADAS

Arico Viejo

Villa de Arico

Porís de
Abona

Granadilla

El Médano

Santa Cruz p.26.
From sculptures and shopping to art galleries and nightlife, Tenerife's cosmopolitan capital is a cultural must.

La Laguna and the Anaga p.36.
Architectural treasures abound in this former capital, university town and Unesco World Heritage centre, close to superb hiking in unchanged, wild landscapes of the Anaga.

Candelaria and Güímar p.44.
The spiritual capital of the island, attracting thousands of pilgrims annually to worship the Black Madonna.

Teide and the interior p.90.
Spain's highest mountain and some of the planet's clearest skies in a lunar, lava landscape.

The southeast coast p.84.
Breezy and sunny, this coast is a magnet for surfers, windsurfers and golfers.

*ATLANTIC
OCEAN*

Northern La Gomera p.114.
Unesco-protected ancient laurel rainforest and superb hiking in La Gomera's fertile north.

N

San Sebastián and southern La Gomera p.100.
The little town with a big history and a laidback resort in the sunny south of La Gomera.

| 0 | kilometres | 10 |
| 0 | miles | 5 |

Things not to miss

It's not possible to see everything that the islands of Tenerife and La Gomera have to offer in one trip – and we don't suggest you try. What follows is a selective taste of the islands' highlights, from beneath the sea to the highest peak.

> Garajonay, La Gomera
See page 115
Enjoy superb hiking and lichen-adorned laurel trees in this ancient rainforest – and Unesco World Heritage site – at the top of La Gomera.

< Parque Nacional del Teide
See page 90
A volcano above the clouds is the metaphorical and literal high point of a visit to Tenerife.

∨ Whale- and dolphin-watching
See page 70
The warm coastal waters between Tenerife and La Gomera are rich feeding grounds for resident and migratory whales and dolphins, providing year-round sightings.

< La Laguna
See page 36
Former capital, Unesco World Heritage site and university town where sixteenth-, seventeenth- and eighteenth-century mansions sit cheek-by-jowl with traditional *tascas* (bars selling tapas) and good shopping.

∨ Masca
See page 64
Hidden, rural hamlet tucked into the folds of the Teno mountains with spectacular views, white-knuckle road access and a demanding three-hour hike down its ravine to the sea.

< **The Anaga**
See page 36
Tenerife's best hiking is in this precipitous mountain range, where life has changed little in five centuries.

∨ **La Orotava**
See page 48
Tenerife's most sophisticated town, where fine examples of traditional balconied houses line narrow streets, whose cobbles are decorated with intricate flower carpets during Corpus Christi celebrations (June).

∧ Garachico
See page 60
Once the richest town on the island, much of it was destroyed by an eruption in 1706. Now, it's the island's prettiest town instead, with rock pools hewn from the solidified lava.

◁ Candelaria
See page 44
Nine bronze, larger-than-life statues of the island's former Menceys (kings) guard the plaza outside the basilica which houses the Black Madonna – Patron Saint of the Canary Islands.

∧ **Jardín Botánico**
See page 53
Exotic gardens made up of some 3000 species of plants and trees collected from across Asia and the Americas, originally deposited in Puerto de la Cruz in 1788 to acclimatize before being shipped to Madrid.

∨ **Mirador de Abrante, La Gomera**
See page 118
A vertigo-inducing skywalk high above the village of Agulo, with views to Mount Teide on the horizon. Good food and demonstrations of *silbo*, the island's whistling language.

∧ **Cliffs of Los Gigantes**
See page 68
The 500m-high, sheer
Acantilados de Los Gigantes
(cliffs of the giants) provide the
most spectacular setting of all
Tenerife's resorts.

< **Drago Milenario, Icod de
los Vinos**
See page 66
Legends and tales surrounding
the island's "dragon trees" are as
numerous as the crowns on this
venerable specimen, thought to
be in the region of 600 to 1000
years old.

< **Parque García Sanabria,
Santa Cruz**
See page 30
Open-air art gallery and extensive
landscaped gardens provide a
tranquil, green space in the heart
of the capital.

∨ **Stargazing**
See page 98
The sky over Tenerife is
considered to be one of the
three clearest on the planet, with
Parque Nacional del Teide the
best place on the island to enjoy
the celestial show.

THINGS NOT TO MISS

Day One in Tenerife

Los Gigantes. See page 68. Head to the marina for whale-watching trips and stop at El Mirador Archipenque on the road out for views over the town to neighbouring La Gomera.

Santiago del Teide. See page 70. Pop into the Casona del Patio to see the old wine press and try an *arepa* (Venezuelan filled corn cakes) at the kiosk by the picnic zone opposite.

Masca. See page 64. The approach road is a series of cliffside switchbacks – not one for nervous drivers. Wander down the cobbled path all the way to the bottom of the village and look back to best appreciate this unique location.

🍽 Lunch. See page 67. *El Guanche* in Masca village has good, home-cooked vegetarian food and a panoramic terrace.

Garachico. See page 60. Visit Garachico to see the prettiest plaza on Tenerife, with its Moorish styled architecture, neoclassical Town Hall and sandstone *La Quinta Roja* hotel. The little Parque Puerta Tierra houses a toll gate – all that was left of the harbour after the 1706 eruption.

Icod de los Vinos. See page 65. Head to this traditional town's Plaza de la Pila for sixteenth- and seventeenth-century balconied houses and the Malvasia Museum, which has fascinating facts about Shakespeare's favourite tipple, the island's renowned Malvasia wine.

🍽 Dinner. See page 67. Try *Mirador de Garachico*, where the portions are enormous, or the bustling *Pizzeria Rugantino*, where the pizzas are even better with a drizzle of their house-made chilli oil.

Los Gigantes marina and cliffs

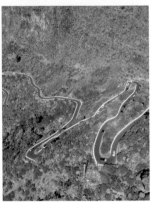
The mountain road to Masca

Iglesia de Nuestra Señora, Garachico

Day Two in Tenerife

La Orotava. See page 48. Climb to the mausoleum in Victoria Gardens for fabulous views over the dome of Iglesia de la Concepción and the red tile rooftops of the old quarter.

El Sauzal. See page 56. Casa Museo de la Sierva de Dios is a tiny museum dedicated to the diminutive Sister María, who was born in the town. She died in 1731 aged 87 and her body has never decayed. A statue of the nun stands outside, making it easy to locate.

 Lunch. See page 59. *Terrazas del Sauzal* has excellent food and, on a clear day, serves up mesmerizing views to Mount Teide.

La Laguna. See page 36. La Laguna's little Sanctuario del Cristo on Plaza del Cristo dates back to the early sixteenth century and holds the most revered statue in the Canary Islands, a Crucifixion sculpted in 1514.

Santa Cruz. See page 26. Passing through Tenerife's capital, pause to look over the sea wall alongside the Auditorium where you'll see a 'gallery' of musician portraits painted on the rocks below. The contemporary display covers everyone from Beethoven to Hendrix.

Las Teresitas. See page 41. A kilometre and a half of golden sand backed by palm trees creates the perfect setting for chilling out after a day of sightseeing. Kiosks at the back of the beach provide chilled beer and snacks.

 Dinner. See page 42. San Andrés, the former fishing village that climbs the ridge behind Las Teresitas, has excellent seafood restaurants. Try *La Posada del Pez* or the more upmarket *Abikore*.

Victoria Gardens, La Orotava

Santuario del Cristo, La Laguna

Musical portraits by the sea, Santa Cruz

A day on La Gomera

An early ferry from Los Cristianos allows a full day for exploring, but roads are so tortuous you'll still only scratch the island's surface.

San Sebastián. See page 100. Don't miss the fifteenth-century Torre del Conde with its small museum in the park of the same name, or the well from which Columbus drew water with which to "baptise the new world", in Casa la Aduana on Plaza de Constitución.

Juego de Bolas Visitor Centre. See page 116. Set within the Parque Nacional de Garajonay, with botanical gardens and displays of artisan crafts as well as information on the park itself.

Mirador de Abrante. See page 118. Just beyond the Juego de Bolas centre, this *mirador* (viewpoint) has a glass platform jutting out over the Abrante cliffs, and views to Mount Teide.

Agulo. See page 118. The island's prettiest and most traditional village, set at the foot of the Abrante cliffs, hemmed in by the *barrancos* (ravines) of Lepe and Las Rosas. On the Eve of San Marcos (April 24), locals jump over juniper wood bonfires.

La Encantadora. See page 116. Beautiful lake set above the town of Vallehermoso, beset with Canarian palm trees. There's a path around the lake and over the dam. You're fairly likely to spot *guaperos* (see page 104) at work in this area, tapping the Canarian pines for their sap in the early morning and late afternoon.

Torre del Conde, San Sebastián

Juego de Bolas centre

La Encantadora

The great outdoors

Away from coastal developments, both Tenerife and La Gomera provide endless opportunities to escape into nature.

The Anaga. See page 36. Step back five centuries to find pockets of local communities clinging to the almost sheer sides of ravines, toiling the Anaga's narrow terraces by hand, and in some cases still living in caves.

Parque Nacional de Garajonay. See page 108. Traverse undulating paths through ancient laurel forests that pre-date the last Ice Age in this Unesco World Heritage site at the top of La Gomera.

The Teno. See page 60. Old merchant trails climb through dense undergrowth and skirt precipitous ridges above deep *barrancos*. Visit in spring to enjoy the mountains at their best.

Botanical Gardens. See page 53. More than three thousand specimens, some of them over 150 years old, crowd into this chaotic gardens. At its heart is a 200-year-old fig tree.

Vallehermoso. See page 115. Some of La Gomera's best hiking is in and around this palm and banana filled valley and its Encantadora (Enchanted) lake.

Barranco del Infierno. See page 79. The most popular hike on Tenerife due to its proximity to southern resorts, a beautiful ravine leads to a waterfall, a rare sight in the south.

Masca Barranco. See page 64. One of the most difficult trails on the island, a three-hour hike down a rocky ravine takes hikers to a small beach from where a boat returns them to Los Gigantes.

The Anaga

Cumbre de Chijeré, Vallehermoso

Hiking in Barranco de Masca

A family day out

With endless beaches and numerous theme parks, kids need never be bored.

Siam Park. See page 76. This Thai-themed water park offers top-notch rides, from a gentle float down a lazy river to the white knuckle Tower of Power that plummets a near-vertical 28m.

Loro Parque. See page 49. Zoological park set within extensive palm groves, run by a foundation which has made a considerable investment in conservation. It's a shame, then, that they still keep captive cetaceans.

Parque Las Águilas – Jungle Park. See page 78. A bobsleigh ride and a live birds of prey show are the highlights of this expansive zoological park in the hills above Los Cristianos. Sadly, they also have performing sea lions.

Whale- and dolphin-watching. See page 70. There's little that compares with the thrill of seeing cetaceans in the wild and sightings here are almost guaranteed as the coastal waters are home to resident pods of bottle-nosed dolphins and pilot whales.

Lago Martiánez. See page 53. César Manrique-designed swimming pool complex in Puerto de la Cruz with seven pools and a vast lake below which the town's casino lies.

Submarine Safari. See page 87. Dive 30m beneath the waves to see the rich variety of tropical fish that occupy the coastal waters off Tenerife, including rays. The battery-operated subs are environmentally sound.

Las Águilas Jungle Park

Lago Martiánez

Submarine Safari

Tenerife off the beaten track

Despite the island's year-round popularity, you don't actually have to travel far to escape the crowds.

El Sauzal. See page 56. A plethora of restaurants, a wine museum and cliff-side gardens are just some of the attractions of this northern hill town lying far below the visitor radar.

Vilaflor. See page 90. Birthplace of Tenerife's only saint and starting point for hiking to Paisaje Lunar, this traditional village set on the edge of the pine forest is just a blur through the coach window for visitors en route to Parque Nacional del Teide.

Candelaria. See page 44. Thousands of pilgrims flock here every August to watch a re-enactment of the finding of the Black Madonna, but few visitors ever see the impressive basilica or its bronze guardians.

San Andrés. See page 40. A small fishing village huddled into the folds of the Anaga just 8km north of Santa Cruz, with some of the best fish and seafood restaurants on the island and the magnificent Las Teresitas beach at its feet. Amazingly, hardly any visitors ever come here.

San Miguel. See page 85. Above the southeast coast, far enough away from the teeming resorts to be nicely off the tourist trail yet still happily situated in the south of the island to make the most of the sunshine hours, this traditional town has bags of character, a nice old quarter, a good choice of restaurants and hiking paths aplenty straight from the door.

Casa del Vino, El Sauzal

Vilaflor

San Andrés

PLACES

Teleférico del Teide

Santa Cruz

Santa Cruz is where, in 1494, Spanish Conquistador Alonso de Lugo planted the holy cross from which the city received its name. Capital of Tenerife since 1723, the city is a popular cruise destination and offers a good blend of green spaces, colonial architecture and culture, all easily explored on foot. The striking Auditorio announces Santa Cruz to those arriving by sea, while Plaza de España provides the central focus for residents and visitors alike. Street art is a prominent feature of the city, particularly along the pedestrianised Calle la Marina, on La Rambla and in Parque Garcia.

Tenerife Espacio de las Artes (T.E.A.)

MAP P.28, POCKET MAP C3
Avda de San Sebastián 10, ⓦ teatenerife. es. Tue–Fri noon–8pm Sat & Sun 10am–8pm. Free entry to the centre, cinema screenings €4, some exhibitions are ticketed.

Tenerife Espacio de las Artes (or **T.E.A.**) is a contemporary art and photography museum, cinema and library housed in a superb example of modern architecture where diagonal surfaces intertwine creating a feeling of endless, interconnected space. There's a permanent exhibition of works by **Oscar Dominguez**, the surrealist artist born in La Laguna, as well as regular temporary exhibitions and arthouse film screenings (in original language).

Museo de la Naturaleza y Arqueología (MUNA)

MAP P.28, POCKET MAP C3
C/Fuente Morales ⓦ museosdetenerife. org. Mon–Sat 9am–7pm, Sun & festivals 10am–5pm. €5.

Housed in an eighteenth-century former hospital building, the city's premier museum, the **Museo de la Naturaleza y Arqueología** (Museum of Nature and Archaeology) contains informative and well-constructed displays on Canarian natural history and archaeology. The most fascinating exhibits relate to the Guanches, with examples of their pottery, tools and rock art all displayed, though most memorable are the gruesome mummified bodies and collection of skeletons.

Arrival and information

Santa Cruz's **bus and tram station** is south of the centre, around ten minutes' walk from the seafront Plaza de España; buses arrive here from almost every corner of the island and trams from La Laguna terminate here. If you're arriving by car, head to the bus station (alongside El Corte Inglés) and leave your vehicle in the underground **car park** – parking in side-streets can be a stressful waste of time. The city's **tourist office** (Mon–Fri 9am–5pm, Sat 9am–2pm; ⓦ elcorazondetenerife.com), located beside the man-made lake at Plaza de España, supplies free town maps and has information about the rest of the island.

Iglesia de Nuestra Señora de la Concepción

MAP P.28, POCKET MAP D3
Plaza de la Iglesia. Mass: Mon–Sat 9am & 7.30pm; Sun & church hols 9am, 11am, noon, 1pm, 6pm & 8pm; entry 30min before service for confession. Closed to visitors outside these times.

Begun in 1502 and taking over two centuries to complete, the **Iglesia de Nuestra Señora de la Concepción** is Santa Cruz's oldest and most important church and a handy landmark thanks to its tall belltower. The building has been gutted by fire several times, meaning that what remains today dates mostly from the seventeenth and eighteenth centuries. Relics and articles of historic significance kept here include part of the *Santa Cruz de la Conquista* (Holy Cross of the Conquest), which dominates the silver Baroque main altar and gave the city its name. The church also holds the remains of one General Gutierrez, the military commander who successfully repulsed Nelson's attack on the town.

La Noria

MAP P.28, POCKET MAP C3
Dominguez Alfonso.

Ask most *santacruceros* where Dominguez Alfonso is and you'll likely get a blank look, but call it **La Noria** and most will know you are referring to the street that stretches west from the Iglesia de Nuestra Señora de la Concepción and forms the heart of one of the oldest, best-preserved and most colourful parts of the city. Pedestrianized, the area is the city's trendiest bar and restaurant district and gets very busy around midnight at the weekends, plus on Sunday afternoons and summer evenings, when the rooftop bars are a favourite place to catch a breeze.

Plaza de España

MAP P.28, POCKET MAP D3
The city's focal point, particularly during carnival and major *fiestas*, is

Iglesia de Nuestra Señora de la Concepción

the **Plaza de España**, its strikingly eclectic blend of Franco symbolism and urban modernism softened by the large lake fountain (in which it's forbidden to paddle – unless CD Tenerife football club get promoted over rivals Gran Canaria). Steps lead underground to a museum housing the remains of **San Cristóbal castle**, which helped defend the city from Nelson, and the El Tigre cannon which allegedly removed the admiral's right arm.

Museo de Bellas Artes

MAP P.28, POCKET MAP C2
C/José Murphy 12 ☎ 922 60 94 46.
Tues–Fri 10am–8pm, Sat, Sun & festivals 10am–3pm. Free.

Though it also holds an eclectic mix of weapons, coins and sculptures – including a Rodin – the **Museo de Bellas Artes** concentrates mainly on paintings. There's a good selection of Canarian artists on display, plus nineteenth-century landscapes along with some battlefields and religious depictions by old masters such as van Loo and Brueghel.

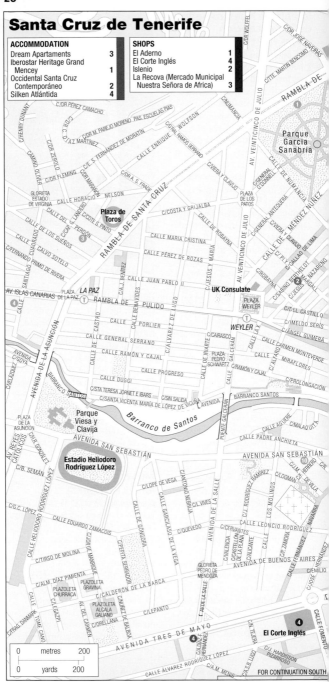

Santa Cruz de Tenerife

ACCOMMODATION		SHOPS	
Dream Apartaments	3	El Aderno	1
Iberostar Heritage Grand		El Corte Inglés	4
Mencey	1	Islenio	2
Occidental Santa Cruz		La Recova (Mercado Municipal	
Contemporáneo	2	Nuestra Señora de Africa)	3
Silken Atlántida	4		

Parque García Sanabria

Plaza de Toros

Plaza DE LOS PATOS

UK Consulate

PLAZA WEYLER

LA PAZ

WEYLER

Parque Viesa y Clavija

Barranco de Santos

Estadio Heliodoro Rodríguez López

El Corte Inglés

| 0 | metres | 200 |
| 0 | yards | 200 |

FOR CONTINUATION SOUTH

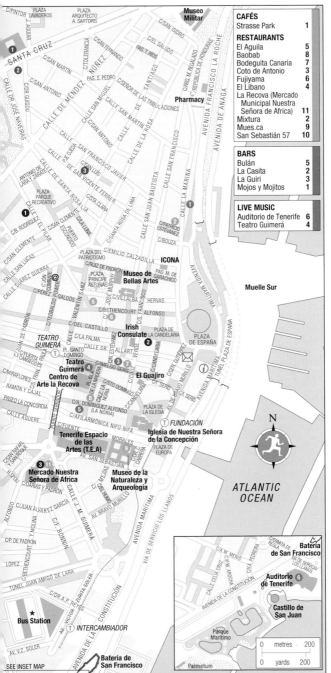

CAFÉS
Strasse Park	1

RESTAURANTS
El Aguila	5
Baobab	8
Bodeguita Canaria	7
Coto de Antonio	3
Fujiyama	6
El Libano	4
La Recova (Mercado Municipal Nuestra Señora de Africa)	11
Mixtura	2
Mues.ca	9
San Sebastián 57	10

BARS
Bulán	5
La Casita	2
La Guiri	3
Mojos y Mojitos	1

LIVE MUSIC
Auditorio de Tenerife	6
Teatro Guimerá	4

Museo Militar

MAP P.28, POCKET MAP D1

C/San Isidro 2 Ⓦ ejercito.defensa.gob.es.
Tues–Fri 9am–3pm, Sat, Sun & festivals
10am–2pm. Free; official photo ID
necessary for admission.

Santa Cruz's **Museo Militar** (Military Museum) has exhibitions on the evolution of weaponry through the ages, but largely focuses on the town's finest military hour – its repulse of the attack by Lord Nelson in 1797 in which the seafaring hero lost not only many of his men, but, more famously, his right arm.

Parque García Sanabria and Rambla de Santa Cruz

MAP P.28, POCKET MAP B1–C2 & A2–D1

The city's two most popular places to stroll away a weekend evening are the grand boulevard **Rambla de Santa Cruz** and the eclectic park at its northern end, the **Parque García Sanabria**. Both are worth a visit at any time of day though to see their collection of open-air modern art sculptures.

Known as the "lungs of the city", Parque García Sanabria has two pieces of sculpture of particular note, *La Fecundidad*, a voluptuous female nude by Frances Borges Salas, and *Monumento al Gato*, by local artist Oscar Dominguez. The landscaping includes a delightful Italian garden, a bamboo tunnel (particularly impressive when the jacaranda petals fall in June) and the flower clock at the Calle Mendez Núñez entrance.

The sculpture trail along the Rambla has been in place since Santa Cruz's 1974 hosting of the first International Street Sculpture Exhibition. Many are now time-worn, though the Henry Moore is as magnificent as ever. Walking along the Rambla, plan for a detour down to the **Plaza Los Patos** to see the Gaudí-style tiled benches.

Auditorio de Tenerife

MAP P.28, POCKET MAP C5

Avda de la Constitución 1
Ⓦ auditoriodetenerife.com.

Nelson's attack on Santa Cruz

In 1797 **Admiral Nelson**, commanding a fleet of eight men o' war, launched a bungling, unsuccessful and ultimately embarrassing attack on Santa Cruz; it cost the lives of many of his men and, more famously, his right arm.

The assault was carried out after four years of war against Spain, with the intention of capturing New World gold from the galleon *San José* that was sheltering in the town's harbour. The battle plan involved the British encircling then invading the town, and Nelson, never one to shrink from the action, was among the second wave of landing craft. He was about to land when he was struck by grapeshot on his right arm, shattering the bone and severing a major artery. By all accounts, Nelson bore this stoically, his first action being to switch his sword to his good hand before returning to his ship and telling the ship's surgeon that the arm had to go, and the sooner the better. Within half an hour of the amputation, the admiral was up, giving orders and practicing his left-handed signature for an ultimatum demanding the town give up the galleon.

The letter would never be sent, however, since by daylight all seven hundred British on shore decided to **surrender**. Nelson left the scene thoroughly frustrated by his misjudgment – though this would be his only military defeat – and depressed that his disablement might spell the end of his naval days – which it didn't.

The plaza fountain

Looking like a huge wave, the head-turning **Auditorio Adán Martín** (known simply as Auditorio de Tenerife) was designed by Calatrava Santiago and provides Santa Cruz with a first-class venue for the arts. The building cleverly plays on a nautical theme, with many of its windows shaped like portholes and the tiny tiles on its bright white exterior shimmering like fish scales. For a glimpse inside you'll have to attend a performance (see page 35).

Castillo de San Juan

MAP P.28, POCKET MAP C5
Avda de la Constitución. Closed to the public.
Also commonly called the Castillo Negro, the **Castillo de San Juan** makes a striking contrast with its neighbour, the Auditorio. This dark, stout little seventeenth-century portside fort once guarded the town's harbour and was also, grimly enough, the site of a bustling trade in African slaves. Unfortunately, it's not open to visitors.

Parque Marítimo

MAP P.28, POCKET MAP B6–C6
Avda de la Constitución 5
ⓦ parquemaritimosantacruz.es. Daily: July & Aug 10am–7pm; Sept–June 10am–6pm. €5, over-65s, retired & under-12s €2.50, under-2s free.
In the absence of a city beach, the **Parque Marítimo** is where Santa Cruz's inhabitants come to take a dip in one of the seawater pools or soak up the sun and the views along the coast. The complex was designed by Canarian artist **César Manrique** – in the same style as the more famous lido in Puerto de la Cruz – and includes the pools, shops, fountains, a restaurant and a sauna. If you'd rather be at a beach, hop on one of the frequent buses (#910) to Playa de Las Teresitas (see page 41).

Palmetum

MAP P.28, POCKET MAP A6–B6
Avda de la Constitución 5 ⓦ palmetum tenerife.es. Daily 10am–6pm. €6, under-12s €2.80, under-2s free.
Over twenty years in the making, the **Palmetum** is a garden of Eden with two thousand species of tropical and subtropical plants, including 400 species of palm trees. Paths wind through the trees and alongside waterfalls and small lakes, affording expansive views over the city. This is a place for quiet contemplation.

Shops

El Aderno

MAP P.28, POCKET MAP C4

C/El Pilar 27 Ⓦ eladerno.com. Daily
9am–9pm, closed 3–4.30pm Mon & Tue.
Hand-made chocolates and cakes
in what began as a small bakery
in Buenavista in 1991 and now
has branches across the island.
Try the mousse mojito or the
truffle chocolate roll – but really,
everything they make here is
delicious.

El Corte Inglés

MAP P.28, POCKET MAP B4–B5

Avda Tres de Mayo 7 Ⓦ elcorteingles.es.
Mon–Sat 9.30am–9.30pm.
Spain's version of Selfridge's
(though it is as ubiquitous as Marks
and Spencer). This comprehensive
department store has an emphasis
on high-quality products and first-
class service. The café at the top has
great city views.

Islenio

MAP P.28, POCKET MAP C3

Plaza de la Candelaria 6 ☎ 922 24 39 32.
Mon–Fri 10am–8.30pm, Sat 10am–8pm.
Well-stocked gift shop selling typical
crafts and produce from across the

Canary Islands, as well as standard
souvenirs and gifts. Also has a good
selection of books, magazines, and
some unusual postcards.

La Recova (Mercado Municipal Nuestra Señora de África)

MAP P.28, POCKET MAP C4

Avda de San Sebastián 51 Ⓦ la-recova.
com. Mon–Sat 6am–2pm, Sun 7am–2pm.
Large, multi-level covered food
market in simple but elegant
Moorish buildings with a bustling
fish market on the lower level.
Great for picking up foodie
souvenirs like local cheeses, wines
and honey. The adjoining shopping
centre is open Mon–Sat 9am–9pm.

Café

Strasse Park

MAP P.28, POCKET MAP B1

C/Celia Cruz 2 Parque García Sanabria
Ⓦ strassepark.es. Daily 9am–midnight.
Trendy, contemporary café and
bistro set alongside the park with
a leafy terrace at treetop level.
Popular venue for cocktails at
sunset and after dark. Try their
saperoco (specialist Tenerife coffee
layered with condensed milk and

La Recova (Mercado Municipal Nuestra Señora de África)

Tapas perfect for sharing

the citrus-flavoured Spanish alcohol Licor 43). £–££

Restaurants

El Aguila

MAP P.28, POCKET MAP C2
Plaza Alféreces Provisionales Ⓦ elaguila
restaurante.com. Daily 9am–midnight.
Popular meeting place with outdoor seating alongside Plaza del Príncipe and an elegant drago tree. The menu is a mix of Canarian and contemporary Asian and internationally-inlfuenced dishes such as bao buns with crab. The lunch menu is updated daily according to seasonal produce available. £

Baobab

MAP P.28, POCKET MAP C3
C/Antonio Dominguez Alfonso 30 Ⓦ baobab
canarias.es. Thu 1–4pm & 8–11.30pm, Fri
& Sat 1pm–midnight, Sun 1–11pm.
One of the best restaurants on La Noria, a refurbished townhouse with a contemporary styled interior and a rooftop terrace (Fri & Sat only, booking recommended). Traditional dishes are given a creative makeover

– try their *queso asado* and their *carrilleras Iberica* (weekends only). £

Bodeguita Canaria

MAP P.28, POCKET MAP C3
C/Imeldo Serís 18, Ⓦ bodeguitacanaria.
com. Mon–Thu & Sat 1–4.30pm & 7–11pm,
Fri 1–11pm, Sun 1–4.30pm.
Well-established and popular with locals and tourists. A great spot to sample a variety of traditional Canarian specialities in small *tapas* portions, though larger dishes are also served. Reasonable prices and an excellent selection of local wines to compliment the food. £

Coto de Antonio

MAP P.28, POCKET MAP A2
C/Perdón 13 ☎ 922 27 21 05. Tue–Sat
1–4pm & 8–11pm, Sun 1–4pm.
Elegant, simply decorated place, more popular with locals than visitors. The excellent menu is based around Basque and Canarian cuisine, with superb and varied daily dishes as well as regular favourites including steak tartare. £–££

Fujiyama

MAP P.28, POCKET MAP A2

C/José Murphy 2 ⓦ restaurante-japones-fujiyama.business.site. Daily 12.30–4.30pm & 7–11.30pm

Japanese food might not seem like the obvious choice in Tenerife, but this restaurant is perfectly placed on the seafront to take advantage of the freshest fish to make traditional Japanese favourites, including a huge selection of sushi and sashimi. It is a marriage made in food heaven. Daily specials and a tasting menu also available. £–££

El Líbano

MAP P.28, POCKET MAP A2
C/Santiago Cuadrado 36 ⓦ restaurante ellibano.com. Daily 1–4pm & 8pm–midnight.

Simple Lebanese restaurant tucked in a side-street and offering old favourites such as kebabs and stuffed vine leaves at reasonable prices, along with more unusual dishes such as *beme* – a traditional vegetable dish – and a superb selection of vegetarian options. £

La Recova (Mercado Municipal Nuestra Señora de África)

MAP P.28, POCKET MAP C4

San Sebastián 57

Avda de San Sebastián 51 ⓦ la-recova. com. Market Mon–Sat 6am–2pm, Sun 7am–2pm; food stalls open lunchtime only, Tues–Sun.

Excellent fish and seafood on offer from a handful of stalls in the lower floor of the market. Top-notch creative cuisine – try the *Bokanka* stall – available alongside more traditional seafood dishes such as ceviche or *boquerones*. £

Mixtura

MAP P.28, POCKET MAP D2
C/Patricio Estevanez 2 ☏ 922 02 26 99. Tues–Thurs 1–4pm & 8–11pm, Fri & Sat 1–4.30pm & 8–11pm, Sun 1–4pm.

Small, friendly restaurant with an eclectic menu of Andalucian/Iberian fusion and a good selection of local wines. Good for *tapas* too. Great seasonal specials include *bacalao* (cod) tempura with Martini mayonnaise. £

Mues.ca

MAP P.28, POCKET MAP C5
C/Fuente Morales (inside MUNA) ⓦ grupo-mag.es/mues-ca. Wed 1–5pm, Thu 1–5pm & 8pm–midnight, Fri 1pm–midnight, Sat 10am–midnight, Sun 10am–6pm.

Swish venue attached to the Museo de Naturaleza y Arqueología offering a range from brunch at weekends or *tapas* in the evening, to a three-course meal with wine. Smaller portions are available for all of the main dishes. Excellent quality for the price. Book ahead if you want to get a table for the popular weekend brunch. £–££

San Sebastián 57

MAP P.28, POCKET MAP B3
Avda de San Sebastián 57 ☏ 822 10 43 25. Mon–Sat 1–5pm & 8pm–midnight.

One of the best contemporary Canarian-cuisine restaurants on the island and for good reason, the food here is exceptionally good. The menu includes delights such as oven fried oysters, *gofio* Chantilly with white chocolate foam and *cherne* ceviche. The six-course tasting menu is a special treat. £££

Bars

Bulán

MAP P.28, POCKET MAP C3
C/ Antonio Domínguez Alfonso 35
Ⓦ bulantenerife.com. Daily noon–1am.
What started life as a chillout bar
now serves a decent food menu too.
It remains a bar at heart though
and a good place to start or end the
night. The imaginative team even
made the best of a difficult situation,
turning coronavirus restrictions into
regular 'masquerade nights'.

La Casita

MAP P.28, POCKET MAP B2
C/Jesús Nazareno 14 ☏ 922 24 78 51. Tue–
Thu 1–11pm, Sat & Sun 1pm–midnight.
Quirky café/bar, less rowdy than
some of the other bars in town, but a
good place to go for quiet drinks on
the terrace. Also serves snacks such
as nachos and sandwiches along with
desserts and coffee. Caters to the
more arty crowd and popular with
the younger local crowd.

La Guiri

MAP P.28, POCKET MAP C3
C/Clavel 9 Ⓦ laguiribar.com Wed & Thu
7pm–midnight, Fri & Sat 7pm –2am, Sun
8pm–midnight
Santa Cruz's party central. One of
the best selections of beers in town
and regular happy hours with 2
for 1 cocktails. You will regularly
find crowds on the dancefloor here
until the early hours. It is definitely
aimed at tourists rather than locals,
but if you are looking for a place to
dance the night away, this is it.

Mojos y Mojitos

MAP P.28, POCKET MAP C3
Avenida Anaga 9 Ⓦ signabailando.com.
Daily 6pm–2am.
Lively café and bar with pleasant
outdoor seating in a new location
since 2021. When the kitchen
closes, the volume and vibe turn up
a notch and it becomes one of the
busiest bars in town. Live music on
occasional summer weekends. Try

Auditorio de Tenerife

their trademark mojitos, especially
during the daily happy hour.

Live music

Auditorio de Tenerife

MAP P.28, POCKET MAP C5
Avda de la Constitución 1 ☏ 922 31 73
27, Ⓦ auditoriodetenerife.com. Ticket
office Mon–Fri 10am–2pm & 5–7pm, Sat
10am–2pm.
This eye-catching venue for the
performing arts has great acoustics
and is home to Tenerife's well-
respected symphony orchestra,
though its progamme of events is
much wider, including jazz, classical
guitar and folk. The Festival de
Música de Canarias in February is
the highlight of the annual calendar.

Teatro Guimerá

MAP P.28, POCKET MAP C3
Plaza Isla de la Madera 2 ☏ 922 60 62 65,
tickets ☏ 902 36 46 03, Ⓦ teatroguimera.es.
Ticket office Tues–Fri 11am–1pm, 6–8pm.
Tenerife's longest-standing
performing arts venue. Its
programme includes classical
music, ballet, opera and theatre
performances.

La Laguna and the Anaga

A good deal cooler and rainier than most of the rest of the island, the university town of La Laguna was Tenerife's first major settlement and, for over two hundred years, its capital. The cultural, religious and academic centre of Tenerife, its well-preserved historic core is a Unesco World Heritage Site and a showpiece of Canarian architecture. During term times, the university district is the busiest area of town, its streets, bars, cafés and bookshops buzzing with activity. Nearby, the volcanic Anaga range, is a rugged landscape of knife-edge ridges surrounded by deep ravines and intermittently coated in rare laurel forests that predate the last Ice Age. Tucked into the folds of the mountains, connected by one sinuous main road, small communities survive on subsistence farming as their ancestors have done for more than five centuries. This remote and dramatic terrain provides Tenerife's most spectacular hiking.

Plaza del Adelantado

MAP P.37

Leafy **Plaza del Adelantado** is at the heart of La Laguna's historic centre and contains the *ayuntamiento* (town hall) and the **Convento Santa Catalina**, built in 1611, whose wooden grille on the upper floor allowed the nuns to watch events in the square below without being seen.

Iglesia de Nuestra Señora de la Concepción

MAP P.37

Plaza de la Concepción 11, La Laguna Ⓦ parroquialaconcepciondelalaguna. wordpress.com. Daily 10am–7.30pm; tower Mon 10am–2pm, Tues–Fri 10am–5pm, Sat 10am–2pm. Free, tower £2.

The island's first church, the **Iglesia de la Concepción**, has evolved over the years in a number of different styles, Gothic being the most evident. Climb to the top of the tower for 360-degree views across the city and Valle de Aguere.

Teatro Leal

MAP P.37

C/Obispo, La Laguna Ⓦ teatroleal.es. Ticket office Mon–Sat 11am–1pm & 6–8pm.

Performances individually priced.

Constructed in 1915, the ornate **Teatro Leal** is the work of architect Antonio Leal Martin and is eclectic in style. The building rises four floors, and inside has a horseshoe-shaped floor. A varied programme of dance, theatre and musical performances is staged here.

Santa Iglesia Catedral

MAP P.37

Plaza de Nuestra Señora de los Remedios, La Laguna ☎ 922 25 91 30, Ⓦ lalagunacatedral.com. July & Aug Mon–Fri 10am–8pm, Sat 10am–12.30pm & 2–5pm; Sept–June Mon–Fri 10.30am–6.30pm, Sat 10am–12.30pm & 2–5pm. Tickets can be purchased online in advance, €6

The town's largest church, the **Santa Iglesia Catedral** was only consecrated in 1913. Its interior is a mixture of Baroque and Gothic, the latter seen clearly in the pointed arches of the presbytery and in the decorated windows of the east end. Behind the ornate altar is the tomb of Alonso de Lugo, conqueror of the islands, who died in 1525.

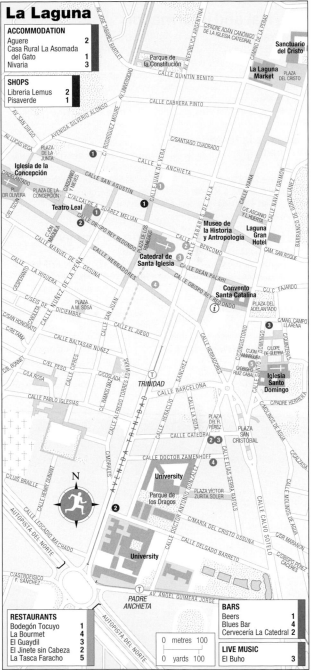

Arrival and information

The **Tranvia** (tram) connects Santa Cruz with La Laguna (every 5min during peak travelling times); the end of the line at La Trinidad is five-minute walk from the old quarter. Buses #14 and #15 from Santa Cruz (every 15min) run to La Laguna's **bus station**, a ten-minute walk southwest of the centre: head along Calle Manuel Hernandez Martín. If arriving by **car**, park on the outskirts and walk in as it's difficult to find a space in the centre.

Museo de la Historia y Antropología

MAP P.37
C/San Agustín 22, La Laguna
Ⓦ museosdetenerife.org. Mon–Sat 9am–7pm, Sun & festivals 10am–5pm. €5.
Housed in the sixteenth century Palacio del Lercaro, the **Museo de la Historia y Antropología** chronicles social and economic development of the Canaries over five centuries and the building alone is worth the entrance fee.

Plaza del Cristo

MAP P.37
Plaza del Cristo, La Laguna. Market Daily 7am–2pm. Santuario daily 8am–1pm & 4–9pm. Free.
The plaza is home to the city's **Mercado Municipal** which is crammed with fresh produce, spices, wines and local specialities. Across the other side of the plaza is the small **Santuario del Cristo**, which contains the oldest and most revered statue in the Canary Islands, a Crucifixion dating from 1514.

Cruz del Carmen

MAP P.40
Buses #76, #77, #273 or #275 from La Laguna, 10–15 daily, 25min.
Cruz del Carmen is a good gateway to Anaga region as it's easily accessed by bus. As well as the car park (beware of theft from cars here), there's the Mirador de Cruz del Carmen (although with frequent low cloud there's often little to see), a restaurant, a small walk to **Los Llanos de los Viejo**

Cruz del Carmen. Anaga

picnic zone and a visitor centre (daily 9am–4pm; ☎922 63 35 76), which can supply a map showing walks hereabouts.

A good **hike** from here (12.4km/3hr 30mins circuit), with excellent views from the outset, leads north through laurel forest and along ridges to the hamlet of Chinamada. To return, consider hiking back along the quiet road from Chinamada to **Las Carboneras** before either heading back to Cruz del Carmen the way you came, or extending the hike to **Taborno**, the village on the opposite side of the valley, where you can walk around the imposing volcanic rock monolith, the **Roque de Taborno**. This adds another two or three hours to the hike.

Almáciga

Almáciga

MAP P.40
Bus #946 from Santa Cruz, 6–8 daily, 50min.

Almáciga – terminus of the bus from Santa Cruz – is a useful point of access for **Playa de San Roque** and **Playa de Benijo**. Both of these beaches are popular with local surfers – high winds along this coast can make for awe-inspiring breakers – and have a few bars and restaurants.

Benijo and El Draguillo hike

MAP P.40
The sealed road from Almáciga ends at the tiny village of **Benijo**. From here a dirt road continues 2km east along the coast to the village of **El Draguillo** – so called for its dragon tree forest – where the path splits. The coastal trail (a 6km return hike) heads east to the **Faro de Anaga**, the island's oldest lighthouse perched 237m above sea level on the cliffs above Roque Bermejo via the scenic village of **Las Palmas** and within sight of the bird reserve **Roque de Dentro**, while the route heading inland climbs steeply to Chamorga. The two can be made into an 11km loop; if you do this, it's best to head

in an anti-clockwise direction first to get all the climbing out of the way early on.

Chamorga

MAP P.40
Bus #947 from Santa Cruz, 3 daily, 1hr 10min.

Chamorga is a small, well-kept village spread across a valley that's studded with palms and dotted with neat terraces. The village is an easy day-trip from Santa Cruz and gives access to some of the best walks in the region. One good **hike** (7km/3hr) follows a loop from Chamorga east down the valley to a small cluster of houses near Roque Bermejo, a sharp spit of land in the sea only accessible on foot, or by boat from San Andrés (€40 round trip, online advance booking essential – ⊕ nauticanivaria. com). From here you climb back to Chamorga by way of a well-graded ridge walk that starts near the **Faro de Anaga** (see page 39). For a **longer loop** (14km/7hr) hike north to El Draguillo and then east along the remote coastal path to the lighthouse before completing the loop to Chamorga via either the valley or ridge.

Chinamada

MAP P.40

Known for its houses built in natural caves in the rock (it even has a traditional restaurant in a cave), the hamlet of **Chinamada** has some of the most spectacular views in the region and an excellent hike brings you here from Cruz del Carmen (see page 38). The panorama from the **Mirador Aguaide** (just beyond the village; accessed via an obvious track beside the town plaza) is particularly dizzying. From here, a steep and mountainous trail takes hikers down to the unattractive and sleepy town of **Punta del Hidalgo** (4.7km/2hr 10mins) to catch buses back to Santa Cruz (#105 every 30min, 1hr 10min) or La Laguna (#224 six daily, 1hr 35min; #50 Sat & Sun every 30min, 35min). This route can also be done in reverse – though it's all climbing – to Cruz del Carmen (around 5hr).

San Andrés

MAP P.40

Buses #910, #945 & #946 from Santa Cruz, frequent, 20min.

Despite only being around the headland from Santa Cruz, **San Andrés** feels like a different world. A cluster of white houses huddle between the confluence of two *barrancos,* at their feet a shanty town of fishermen's huts which border Playa de las Teresitas. Alongside San Andrés are the remains of a small castle, La Torre de San Andrés, that played an important role in Santa Cruz against the attack by Nelson and is now appropriately known as El Castillo Roto (The Broken Castle). Under near constant attack from corsairs in the sixteenth- and seventeenth-centuries, the village was known as "the pirate port". Water-rich from its *barrancos*, the village once provided so much produce for Santa Cruz that it was

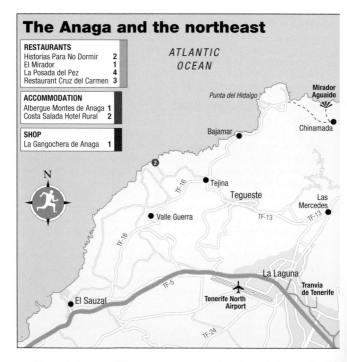

The Anaga and the northeast

RESTAURANTS
Historias Para No Dormir 2
El Mirador 1
La Posada del Pez 4
Restaurant Cruz del Carmen 3

ACCOMMODATION
Albergue Montes de Anaga 1
Costa Salada Hotel Rural 2

SHOP
La Gangochera de Anaga 1

ATLANTIC OCEAN

Mirador Aguaide

Punta del Hidalgo

Chinamada

Bajamar

N

Tejina

Teguestte

Las Mercedes

TF-16

TF-13

TF-13

Valle Guerra

TF-16

TF-5

La Laguna

Tranvía de Tenerife

El Sauzal

Tenerife North Airport

TF-24

known as the city's larder. Today it's a favourite lunch venue for *santacruceros* who come to enjoy its fine fish and seafood restaurants.

Playa de las Teresitas

MAP P.40

Buses #910, #945 & #946 from Santa Cruz, frequent, 20min.

Below the leafy hillside village of San Andrés, the large artificial **Playa de las Teresitas** was created in 1973 using millions of tonnes of sand from the former Spanish Sahara in order to provide *santacruceros* with a beach escape beside the towering Anaga mountains. A large man-made breakwater eliminates waves and currents around the palm-studded sand, and good facilities make it a pleasant place for a day of sunbathing. If it's a breezy day, the fine texture of the sand means sunbathers may receive an unexpected sand-exfoliation.

Playa de las Gaviotas

MAP P.40

Bus #945 from Santa Cruz, 9 daily, 20min.

The next cove east after Las Teresitas, **Playa de las Gaviotas** is named after the seagulls that frequent it and is a much quieter stretch, popular with nudists. A bar on the front serves snacks and drinks (Wed–Sun, high season only).

Taganana

MAP P.40

Bus #946 from Santa Cruz, 6–8 daily, 45min.

Taganana is a tiny town in a magnificent setting that began as a sugar cane centre before moving into wine production. Precariously sprawled over ridges and hillsides, it was long remote from the rest of Tenerife and is worth a stroll for its narrow streets, old Canarian houses and its 1505 **church**, Iglesia de Nuestra Señora de las Nieves, one of the oldest in the Canary Islands.

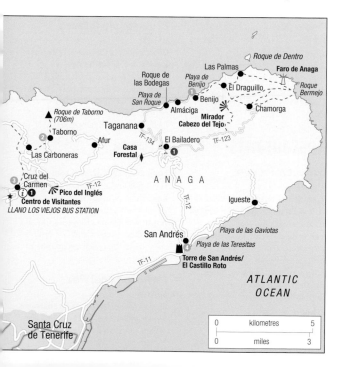

Shops

La Gangochera de Anaga

MAP P.40

Rctra Monte De Las Mercedes, Cruz Del Carmen; Buses #76, #77, #273 Or #275 From La Laguna, 10–15 Daily, 25min ☎ 922 26 42 12. Daily 9am–5pm.

Small shop/café alongside the car park where you can enjoy snacks and delicious homemade cakes as well as picking up a good selection of detailed maps, reference books (in Spanish), fruit and artisan produce such as honey and cheeses.

Librería Lemus

MAP P.37

C/Heraclio Sánchez 64, La Laguna ⓦ librerialemus.com. Mon–Fri 9.30am–1.30pm & 4–8pm, Sat 9.30am–1.30pm.

Tenerife's best bookshop, this place has an extensive range of titles – including a useful local travel section – though most are in Spanish. The stationary section is a good place to find gifts.

Pisaverde

MAP P.37

C/Juan de Vera 7, La Laguna ⓦ pisaverdestore.com Mon–Sat 10am–8pm.

Hip, colourful and eco-conscious shoes and boots from this artisan Tenerife designer. Every shoe, they claim, is unique.

Restaurants

Bodegón Tocuyo

MAP P.37

C/Juan de Vera 16, La Laguna ☎ 922 25 00 45. Mon–Sat noon–3pm & 7pm–midnight.

A dark-wood, traditional *tasca* with graffitied walls and barrels for tables, this is easily the town's most atmospheric place for *tapas* and wine. Try the *tablas* of Iberico and cheese and their *almogrote*, a pungent cheese paste from La Gomera. £

La Bourmet

MAP P.37

C/Herrederos 46, La Laguna ⓦ labourmet.com. Sun–Thurs 1–11.30pm, Fri & Sat 1–midnight.

Quality burger and coffee bar, popular with locals. Burgers are made to order – there's not a whiff of fast food about the place. They also have artisan beers and ciders. £

El Guaydil

MAP P.37

C/Dean Palahi 26, La Lagua ☎ 822 04 76 65. Mon–Thu 1.30–4pm & 7–10pm, Fri 1.30–10pm, Sat 1.30–4pm & 8–10.30pm.

A wide variety of *tapas* and typical Canarian pork dishes served up in a rustic but contemporary décor. £

Historias Para No Dormir

MAP P.40

Lugar Caserío Taborno 0, Taborno ☎ 922 69 02 27. Thurs–Sun 8am–6.45pm.

Located in the tiny rural hamlet of Taborno, from the outside it looks like any number of local restaurants, but the menu reveals French influences and some unusual ingredients such as wild boar and kangaroo. A three-course lunch. £

El Jinete sin Cabeza

MAP P.37

C/Bencomo 23, La Laguna ☎ 622 88 62 88. Tues–Sat 1–4pm (lunch only).

Popular, bijou restaurant with a small menu of Spanish and Canarian fusion dishes, nicely prepared and presented using all local produce and including vegetarian options. £

El Mirador

MAP P.40

Benijo ☎ 627 29 55 42. Daily noon–5.30pm.

Fresh fish and seafood served with a tad more panache than in other nearby restaurants. Its clifftop position overlooks Playa Benijo and the northeast coast and is a distance away from the coach excursions in Roque de las Bodegas. £

La Posada del Pez

MAP P.40

Ctra San Andres-Taganana 2 ⓦ restaurante laposadadelpez.com. Tues 1–4.40pm, Wed & Thurs 1–4.30pm & 7–11pm, Fri–Sat 1–11pm, Sun 1–4.30pm.

San Andres is full of good fish and seafood restaurants, but *La Posada* is a cut above. It's considered one of the best fish and seafood restaurants on Tenerife – with prices to match. Reservations are recommended. ££

Restaurant Cruz del Carmen

MAP P.40

Ctra General La Mercedes ☎ 922 25 00 62. Mon–Wed & Fri 11am–6pm, Sat & Sun 9am–6pm.

Good, basic traditional cuisine: try the *cabrito frito* (fried goat) or the *conejo en salmorejo* (rabbit stew). Makes a welcome sanctuary for hikers when the Anaga cloud descends. Very busy with Canarian hikers on weekends. £

La Tasca Faracho

MAP P.37

C/Santo Domingo 26, La Laguna ☎ 922 26 32 80. Sun & Tue 1–4pm, Wed–Sat 1–4pm & 8–11pm.

A local favourite for *tapas* and wine at reasonable prices. A decent cheese selection is also available to eat in or take away. This is also a good place to get stocked up on bottles of wine from across the Canaries. The owners are knowledgeable and helpful. £

Bars

Beers

MAP P.37

C/Alcalde Alonso Suárez Melián 21, La Laguna ☎ 646 76 79 71. Tue–Thu & Sun 2–4pm & 8–11pm, Fri & Sat 2–4pm & 8pm–midnight.

Bright, contemporary bar named in homage to *Cheers* stocking a wide range of bottled and craft beers from around the world. They also do great burgers. Vegetarian and vegan options too.

Blues Bar

MAP P.37

C/Dr. Zamenhoff 9, La Laguna ☎ 922 63 35 35. Thu–Sat 10.30pm–3.30am.

An alternative to Latino and Spanish sounds, although you're as likely to hear jazz or swing at the *Blues Bar*. Some say it's the best bar in the *cuadrilátero*, the triangle where the most popular bars are located. Drinks only.

Cervecería La Catedral

MAP P.37

C/Catedral 3, La Laguna ☎ 664 43 82 46. Daily 4pm–2am.

Hugely popular beer and sausage bar, in business for over thirty years and still going strong – though you can expect a wait for your food. Try the metre-long sausage, chips and salad for the table, washed down with draft German beer by the litre.

Live music

El Buho

MAP P.37

C/Catedral 3, La Laguna ☎ 686 47 93 88. Thurs–Sun 7pm–3.30am.

Pub, club and one of La Laguna's few dependable live-music venues. Rock bands or tribute acts on intermittent Fridays and Saturdays. For gig details look out for posters along C/Doctor Antonio or check the Facebook page. Entrance fee.

La Laguna tapas bar and restaurant

Candelaria and Güímar

Though easily bypassed on the main TF-1 motorway from Santa Cruz to the southern resorts, the barren landscape of Tenerife's east coast does contain two outstanding attractions – the Basilica at Candelaria, considered the holiest site in the Canary Islands, and the Pirámides de Güímar, one of the island's most controversial sites. As Tenerife's Lourdes, Candelaria is well set up for day-trippers (Güímar rather less so), though the Puertito de Güímar – its coastal outpost – has a couple of good seafood restaurants and a nice hike across the malpaís (volcanic badlands).

Basilica de Nuestra Señora de Candelaria

MAP P.44

Plaza Patronata de la Candelaria. Buses #120, #121, #122, #123, #124, #126, #127 or #131 from Santa Cruz, 21 daily, 30min ☏ 922 50 01 00. Mon 3–7.30pm,

Tues–Sun 7.30am–7.30pm. Free.
West of Santa Cruz stretches a string of dormitory settlements that peter out around **Candelaria**, a largely avoidable town were it not for the **Basilica de Nuestra Señora de Candelaria**. Housing a famous

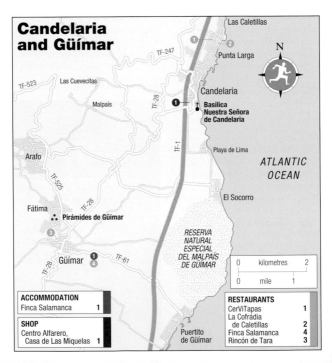

Candelaria and Güímar

Las Caletillas

TF-247

Punta Larga

TF-523

Las Cuevecitas

Candelaria

Malpaís

TF-28

❶ ✝ **Basilica Nuestra Señora de Candelaria**

Arafo

TF-1

Playa de Lima

ATLANTIC OCEAN

TF-525

Fátima

TF-28

❇ **Pirámides de Güímar**

El Socorro

❸

Güímar

TF-28

TF-61

RESERVA NATURAL ESPECIAL DEL MALPAÍS DE GÜÍMAR

| 0 | kilometres | 2 |

| 0 | mile | 1 |

Puertito de Güímar

ACCOMMODATION	
Finca Salamanca	1

SHOP	
Centro Alfarero, Casa de Las Miquelas	1

RESTAURANTS	
CerViTapas	1
La Cofrádia de Caletillas	2
Finca Salamanca	4
Rincón de Tara	3

The Guanches

Tenerife's original inhabitants, the **Guanches**, were tall, powerfully built, fair-skinned people. They lived in caves and were primarily **hunter-gatherers.** With no naturally occurring metals on the island, they lived a Stone-Age life right up until the Spanish conquest in 1494. Similarities in ceramics, language and culture suggest that the Guanche were of **Amazigh (Berber) origin**, probably from the High Atlas Mountains in Morocco – but with no boat building skills, how they got to the islands remains a mystery.

In contrast to their fairly basic technology, the Guanche had a complex **society**. Both Tenerife and La Gomera were divided into several *menceyatos* (kingdoms) – the names of which survive as modern place-names, including Anaga, Tegueste, Tacaronte, Taoro, Icod, Adeje, Abona, Güímar – which often warred with one another. Each community had three classes of society: the monarchy, a nobility and the remaining population (mainly peasants, craftsmen and goatherds). The rank of nobility – which bestowed to men the right to grow long hair – was attained not through birth but as a result of personal qualities or actions.

The Guanche were a **religious** and deeply superstitious people, who worshipped a single god, Achaman, to whom animal sacrifices and libations were made and whose physical manifestation was thought to be the sun. His opposite number was Guayota, a devil that dwelt in hell, Echeyde, within the crater of Mount Teide – and who punished misdeeds through volcanic eruptions. Other than building stepped **pyramids**, as at Güímar, the most significant Guanche religious practice was the **mummification** of their nobility. Nobles were buried in caves along with their possessions, particularly their *pintadera*, a person's unique wooden seal worn on a leather thong necklace and thought to be useful in the afterlife.

The role of **women** in Guanche society was strong, for the most part due to a hereditary practice in which monarchic titles transferred through the female line. Women could also hold jobs and are known to have been priests, doctors, potters and warriors.

statue of the Virgin Mary known as the Black Madonna, the patron saint of the Canary Islands, this is the archipelago's most important religious site.

The Virgin (a wooden statue probably from the prow of a wrecked ship) washed up here in the 1390s. Initially kept in a cave and worshipped by the local Guanches, it passed into Spanish hands after the conquest. Though the original was swept out to sea by a tidal wave in 1826, a replica now forms the centrepiece of this splendid late nineteenth-century colonial-style basilica. For the **Feast of the Assumption** (Aug 15th), the re-enactment of the finding of the Virgin attracts pilgrims from across the Canary Islands. Outside the church, the waterfront plaza is guarded by nine bronze statues of the former Guanche *menceyes* (kings), the work of local sculptor José Abad.

Güímar Malpaís

MAP P.44

Hot and dry with a default setting of windy, the central east coast of Tenerife is a near-desert

Pirámides de Güímar

you across the *malpaís* as far as **El Socorro** where the Virgin was first washed up (up to 6km/1hr 50min return).

Pirámides de Güímar

MAP P.44
C/Chacona. Bus #121 or #124 from Santa Cruz to Güímar, 15–23 daily, 45–50min Ⓦ piramidesdeguimar.es. Daily 10am–6pm. €12.50, children (age 7–12) €5.50 pyramids only, other packages are available.

The once thriving agricultural town of **Güímar** is best known as the location of the **Pirámides de Güímar**. Believed by Thor Heyerdahl to have been built by the Guanche, they were long dismissed as piles of stones heaped by farmers clearing the land. However, close inspection by archaeologists revealed three pyramidal constructions, each at least 100 metres long and made of carefully squared stones laid out with considerable geometric exactitude. The structures point to the location of the sun during the winter and summer solstices and the stairs up each flat-topped pyramid face the rising sun. Reconstructed to what is thought to be their original form, the site includes a **museum**, full-sized reed ships and a fascinating short film about Heyerdahl's life.

environment known as *malpaís* (literally 'badlands'). Hosting some of the island's best examples of endemic euphorbias (spurges) such as sweet tabaiba and cardón, it looks barren but this land is home to 150 species of flora and sixty types of butterfly, as well as large colonies of lizards. Flat and easy to walk, the best way to explore the area is on foot. A clearly waymarked path begins from Calle Marques at the eastern edge of El Puertito de Güímar and takes

Thor Heyerdahl

The Norwegian ethnographer **Thor Heyerdahl** came to Tenerife in 1990 to inspect what appeared to be ancient stepped pyramids discovered on the island. Finding them identical to those of Peru, Mexico and Ancient Mesapotamia, he concluded that they could represent a missing link in his theory of **ancient migratory routes** from Southeast Asia to the South Pacific. Teaming up with shipping magnate Fred Olsen to clear the area, restore the pyramids and create an ethnographic park to showcase his theories, Heyerdahl brought Aymara natives from Bolivia to build a replica of the Ra II reed ship on which he famously crossed the Pacific in 1947. Controversy continues to surround the pyramids, with locals still insisting the stones were cleared by farmers and the scientific world still sceptical about Heyerdahl's theories.

Shop

Centro Alfarero, Casa de Las Miquelas

MAP P.44

Isla de la Gomera 7, Candelaria; climb the steps behind the basilica ☎ 922 50 52 16. Tues–Sat 11am–5.30pm. Free.

A small pottery where they still throw pots by hand using local red clay. Small items of ceramics, crafts and jewellery for sale, which make lovely souvenirs.

Restaurants

CerViTapas

MAP P.44

Rambla de los Menceyes 27, Candelaria ☎ 922 19 73 65 Daily noon–11pm.

Modern restaurant serving gourmet *tapas* such as rabbit meatballs and fish and chips, along with Spanish and Tenerife wines and speciality beers. The cheese and meat platter is highly recommended. £

La Cofrádia de Caletillas

MAP P.44

Avda Maritima 31, Candelaria ☎ 922 50 05

Finca Salamanca

01. Sun, Mon & Thurs 1–11pm, Fri & Sat 1–11.30pm.

Fishermen's guild restaurants are usually reliable for good fresh fish and seafood, and this one opposite the harbor is no exception. Very busy with locals at weekends. Catch of the day is sold by the kilo. £

Finca Salamanca

MAP P.44

Ctra Güímar, El Puertito 1.5km, Güímar ☎ 922 51 45 30, Ⓦ en.hotelfincasalamanca. com. Sun–Thu 1.30–4pm & 7–10pm, Fri & Sat 1.30–4pm & 7–10.30pm.

Smart restaurant in a former tobacco drying room in a lovely, traditional rural hotel. Modernised Canarian dishes such as *gofio* pasta with a *puchero* sauce and roast pork in *retama* honey sauce. £

Rincón de Tara

MAP P.44

C/Imeldo Seris 2, Güímar ☎ 670 34 12 09. Tues–Thu 1–4.30pm & 8–11pm, Fri & Sat 1–4.30pm & 8–11.30pm Sun 1–4.30pm.

Colourful take on Canarian/ Spanish cuisine with dishes as attractive as the rustic, casually chic decor. Try the fried El Hierro cheese with *guayaba* jam. £

HOTEL RURAL

Finca Salamanca

Puerto de la Cruz and around

With its lively restaurant scene and leafy plazas, Puerto de la Cruz offers a taste of *tinerfeño* life, successfully combining the traditions and culture of a Canarian working town with the amenities of a holiday resort. Originally a small fishing village, the town became a fashionable spa in the 1890s, favoured by scientists, explorers and dignitaries such as Winston Churchill and Agatha Christie; when Tenerife South airport opened in 1978, siphoning mass tourism south, Puerto was left to its loyal, return visitors. The most fertile area of Tenerife, La Orotava has been highly prized since the Spanish arrived in 1497, when it was gifted to wealthy merchants in exchange for them financing the conquest. Today its eponymous town remains Tenerife's most sophisticated, best known for its Doce Casas – twelve striking Canarian-style mansions that were former residences of the area's leading families – and its magnificent Corpus Christi flower carpets (May/June).

Plaza del Charco

MAP P.50

Prior to the eighteenth century, spring tides often deposited a pool of shrimps in the centre of Puerto de la Cruz's main plaza, giving it its Sunday-best name of **Plaza del Charco de los Camarones**. Today it's the cultural and social epicentre of Puerto. Its giant Indian laurel trees were brought from Cuba in 1852 and now provide welcome shade for the restaurants that ply their trade from the eighteenth-century balconied houses lining its western flank. The focal point for locals, many of the town's main festivals are staged here, including nightly open-air parties during its week long, annual **carnival** (Feb/March).

Casa de la Aduana

MAP P.50

C/Lonjas, Puerto de la Cruz ☎ 922 38 14 90. Mon–Thu & Sat 10am–2pm, Fri 10am–2pm & 5–7.30pm. Free.

Set on the picturesque harbour, the town's oldest building and former customs house of **Casa de la Aduana** was built in 1620. Now housing the town's **tourist office** and traditional crafts and souvenirs shop, it also hosts photographic exhibitions. Behind it lie steps leading to the eighteenth-century ramparts and **Batteria de Santa Barbara**.

Arrival and information

Buses arrive at Puerto de la Cruz's station on C/Hermanos Fernández Perdigon, on the western side of the town centre. Although refurbished in 2019, you may still find that many buses drop off and pick up outside the terminal, rather than navigate their way inside. The **tourist office** (Daily 9am–8pm; ☎922 38 60 00) is in the Casa de la Aduana.

La Ranilla

La Ranilla

MAP P.50

Museum: C/Lomo 9a, Puerto de la Cruz Ⓦ laranilla.org. Mon–Sat 10am–2pm & 5–8pm, Sun 10am–1pm. €2.

Spreading west from the harbour, between Calle Mequinez and Calle del Lomo, is the former fishing quarter and now gastronomic district of **La Ranilla**. The town's best restaurants are to be found along its cobbled streets where tables and chairs are packed on warm evenings. Raise your eyes from the alluring menus to take in the district's local artwork, adorning the gable ends of buildings – some fifteen murals in all. Also here is the **Museo Arqueológico**, which contains a modest collection of Guanche pottery and replicas of some mummified body parts.

Playa Jardín

MAP P.50

Running for almost a kilometre on the western edge of Puerto de la Cruz, the black-sand **Playa Jardín** is the town's premier beach, backed by gardens designed by César Manrique. Spreading all the way to **Punta Brava** (where Loro Parque is located), there are several calmer areas favoured by families and others where the surf is only for those riding boards. A large selection of restaurants and cafés backs the coastline.

Loro Parque

MAP P.50

Avda Loro Parque; free mini-train every 20min from Reyes Católicos (outside Hotel Las Vegas) ☎ 922 37 38 41, Ⓦ loroparque. com. Daily 9.30am–5.30pm (last entry 5pm). €38, under-12s €26.

Tenerife's best-publicized tourist attraction, which has been in operation since 1978. **Loro Parque** zoo's extensive collection includes the world's largest artificial iceberg and its largest collection of parrots, some species of which have been brought back from the brink of extinction by the **Loro Parque Foundation**, which invests heavily in conservation. Unfortunately that work is overshadowed by their continued defence of their **captive cetaceans** programme. They hold dolphin and killer whale performances, which make a sad sight, and have continued breeding captive orcas in spite of a ban.

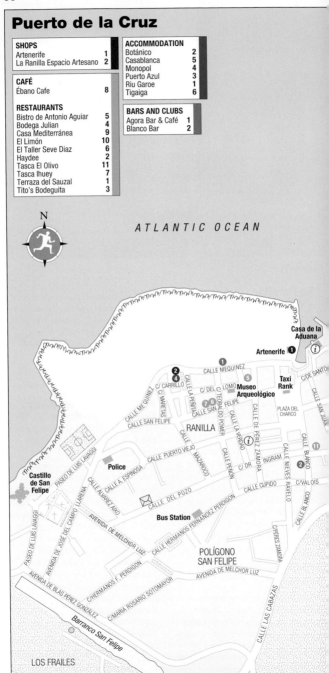

Puerto de la Cruz

SHOPS

Arterenife	1
La Ranilla Espacio Artesano	2

CAFÉ

Ébano Cafe	8

RESTAURANTS

Bistro de Antonio Aguiar	5
Bodega Julian	4
Casa Mediterránea	9
El Limón	10
El Taller Seve Diaz	6
Haydee	2
Tasca El Olivo	11
Tasca Ihuey	7
Terraza del Sauzal	1
Tito's Bodeguita	3

ACCOMMODATION

Botánico	2
Casablanca	5
Monopol	4
Puerto Azul	3
Riu Garoe	1
Tigaiga	6

BARS AND CLUBS

Agora Bar & Café	1
Blanco Bar	2

N

ATLANTIC OCEAN

Casa de la Aduana

Arterenife ❶

CALLE MEQUINEZ

Taxi Rank

C/DE SANTO

CALLE SAN JUAN

❷
❹
C/ CARRILLO
CALLE LA PENITA
C/ DEL LOMO
C/ TEOBALDO POWER

Museo Arqueológico

❺

PLAZA DEL CHARCO

CALLE MEQUINEZ
C/ MARETAS
CALLE SAN FELIPE
❼❻
CALLE SAN FELIPE
CALLE LA VERDA

RANILLA

CALLE DE PEREZ ZAMORA

CALLE PERDON

CALLE NIEVES RAVELO

❶❶

CALLE PUERTO VIEJO

CALLE MAZAROCO

CALLE PERÓN

C/ DR INGRAM

CALLE BLANCO
❷

Police

CALLE A. ESPINOSA

C/VALOIS

PASEO DE LUIS LAVIAGGI

CALLE ALVAREZ AIXO

CALLE CUPIDO

CALLE BLANCO

C/PEREZ ZAMORA

Castillo de San Felipe

CALLE DEL POZO

Bus Station

CALLE HERMANOS FERNANDEZ PERDIGON

PASEO DE LUIS LAVIAGGI

AVENIDA DE JOSE DEL CAMPO LLARENA

AVENIDA DE MELCHOR LUZ

POLÍGONO SAN FELIPE

AVENIDA DE MELCHOR LUZ

AVENIDA DE BLAS PEREZ GONZALEZ

C/HERMANOS F. PERDIGON

C/MARIA ROSARIO SOTOMAYOR

CALLE LAS CABAZAS

Barranco San Felipe

LOS FRAILES

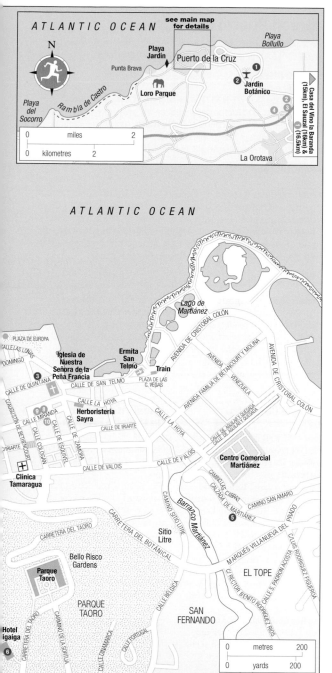

ATLANTIC OCEAN

N

see main map for details

Playa Jardin

Puerto de la Cruz

Playa Bollullo

Punta Brava

Loro Parque

Jardín Botánico

Playa del Socorro

Rambla de Castro

Casa del Vino La Baranda (15km), El Sauzal (16km) & (16.5km)

miles 2

kilometres 2

La Orotava

ATLANTIC OCEAN

Lago de Martiánez

PLAZA DE EUROPA

CALLE LAS LONJAS

DOMINGO

Iglesia de Nuestra Señora de la Peña Francia

Ermita San Telmo

Train

AVENIDA DE CRISTOBAL COLÓN

AVENIDA

AVENIDA FAMILIA DE BETANCOURT Y MOLINA

AVENIDA DE CRISTOBAL COLÓN

CALLE DE QUINTANA

CALLE DE SAN TELMO

PLAZA DE LAS C. VEGAS

CALLE DE AGUILAR Y QUESADA

VENEZUELA

CALLE AGUSTÍN DE BETHENCOURT

CALLE MIRANDA

CALLE LA HOYA

Herboristería Sayra

CALLE DE IRIARTE

CALLE DE ZAMORA

CALLE DE ESQUIVEL

CALLE LA HOYA

CALLE IRIARTE

CALLE COLOGAN

Clinica Tamaragua

CALLE DE VALOIS

CALLE DE VALOIS

Centro Comercial Martiánez

CAMINO LAS CABRAS

CALZADA DE MARTIÁNEZ

CAMINO SAN AMARO

CARRETERA DEL TAORO

CARRETERA DEL TAORO

CAMINO SITIO LITRE

CARRETERA DEL BOTÁNICAL

Barranco Martiánez

Sitio Litre

Bello Risco Gardens

Parque Taoro

PARQUE TAORO

MARQUÉS VILLANUEVA DEL PRADO

EL TOPE

C/ LUIS RODRÍGUEZ FIGUEROA

C/ RECTOR BENITO RODRÍGUEZ RIOS

C/ S. PADRÓN ACOSTA

SAN FERNANDO

CALLE BÉLGICA

CAMINO DE LA SIRILIA

CALLE DINAMARCA

CALLE PORTUGAL

Hotel Taigaiga

metres 200

yards 200

Green Puerto de la Cruz

Considered by botanists to have the perfect climate, Puerto's ebullient foliage provides some excellent **gardens**.

BELLO RISCO
MAP P.50

Carretera Taoro 15 ☎ 922 38 43 71. Temporarily closed at the time of writing. Steps, paths and footbridges weave their way down the cliffside in the lovely water gardens of **Bello Risco**, alongside Parque Taoro, providing a haven for dragonflies and butterflies. The little lakeside café is a delightfully tranquil spot to enjoy afternoon tea.

PARQUE TAORO
MAP P.50

Fronting the former *Taoro* hotel and casino, the stepped terrace gardens of **Parque Taoro** spread down the hillside alongside an impressive waterfall which cascades hourly. At the rear of the hotel and a favourite haunt of joggers, **Parque de la Sortija**, still part of the Parque Taoro area, provides endemic flora set within volcanic *malpaís* and is home to colonies of lizards.

SITIO LITRE
MAP P.50

Camino Sitio Litre ☉ jardineorquideas.com. Mon–Sat 9.30am–2.30pm. €4.50. These delightful orchid gardens surrounding the **Sitio Litre** mansion, have been graced by many a famous guest since their creation in 1774. Most notable are Agatha Christie, who was inspired to create *The Mysterious Mr Quin* while staying at the mansion with her daughter in 1927, and Marianne North, whose paintings of the gardens are part of the Kew Gardens collection.

Rambla de Castro

MAP P.50

Buses #107, #108 #325 and #363 from Puerto de la Cruz, 36–38 daily, 12–25min to Mirador San Pedro (bus stop El Socorro, just beyond)

The lovely, coastal **Rambla de Castro** affords views over Tenerife's most picturesque headland and leads to the small fort of El Fortín and the Casona de Rastro *hacienda* and the ruins of La Gordejuela, Tenerife's first steam engine, dating from 1903. The path starts from alongside the *Hotel Maritim*, which lies on the coast just west of Loro Parque (you can get here using the free mini-train), and can also be accessed from the other end, from the main coastal road at the Mirador San Pedro, where it's clearly signposted.

Iglesia de Nuestra Señora de la Peña Francia

MAP P.50

Plaza de la Iglesia, Puerto de la Cruz ☎ 922 38 00 51. Mass daily 8.30am, 6.30pm & 7pm.

Dominating the elegant plaza named after it, the seventeenth-century **Iglesia de Nuestra Señora de la Peña Francia** is Puerto's main church and one of Tenerife's most beautiful. The statue of the Virgin housed inside wears a cape awarded to Cuban poet María Dulce Loynaz, a frequent visitor and devotee of the town.

San Telmo

MAP P.50

C/San Telmo, Puerto de la Cruz. Free. Founded in 1780 and dedicated to the patron saint of fishermen, the small, white chapel of **San Telmo** once stood within its own battery, and defended the coast against pirates. The victims of a great flood in 1826 are buried beneath its floor.

Lago de Martiánez

MAP P.50

Avda Cristóbal Colón, Puerto de la Cruz
① 922 37 05 72, ⓦ ociocostamartianez.com.
Daily 10am–6pm, 7pm in summer. €5.50
(includes sun lounger; parasol extra).

A beautifully designed open-air saltwater lido, the **Lago de Martiánez** complex contains seven pools including a vast lake beneath which the town's casino is housed. Designed by **César Manrique** (1920–92), the extensive sun terraces are complemented by soft curves and quirky surrealist touches like upside-down trees.

Lago Martiánez

Jardín Botánico

MAP P.50

C/Retama 2 ① 922 92 29 78. Daily
9am–6pm. €3.

In 1788 Carlos III decreed that there should be a space created in Tenerife for "the most unusual plants existing in the Colonies of the Philippines and America" for their acclimatization before onward shipping to the Royal Gardens of Madrid – and so the **Jardín Botánico** was established.

Spanish Conquest

At the dawn of the great age of "discovery" and conquest of sophisticated civilizations around the world by European powers, it surprised Spain to find a Stone-Age culture on its doorstep. Even more of a shock was the struggle conquistadors had to control Tenerife and La Gomera; the islanders, the **Guanches** (see page 45), fought only with weapons made from wood and stone, yet it took the vast majority of the fifteenth century for Spain's crusaders to conquer all of the Canary Islands. **Tenerife** was the last to fall, and even when Columbus sailed past on his famed 1492 voyage it was still in Guanche hands.

Only the following year would the process of conquest begin, and the final defeat of the Guanches didn't come until Christmas Day 1495, at a location now marked by the town La Victoria. At this time Spanish victory was virtually assured since the Guanches had suffered a gigantic epidemic of a **flu** against which they lacked immunity. Of the six hundred Guanche that remained, most were forcibly entered into domestic service or sold as slaves; only a handful, known as Guanches alzados – rebellious Guanches – continued their traditional ways in remote, mountainous areas. Whilst some families claim their bloodlines go back to Guanche, there's no evidence of direct descendants.

Thriving in their new home near Puerto de la Cruz, the first of the specimens shipped to Madrid quickly fell foul of the winter frost there and the project was abandoned – but the gardens remain. Today they are the second-oldest botanical gardens in Spain and include more than 3000 specimens, including 150 different species of palms and an enormous, 200-year-old fig tree.

Casa de los Balcones

MAP P.54

C/San Francisco 3, La Orotava ☎ 922 33 06 29, ⓦ casa-balcones.com. Daily 8.30am–6.30pm. Museum €5.

La Orotava's Calle de San Francisco is known for its impressive seventeenth- and eighteenth-century mansions (known as Doce Casas), the grandest of which is the **Casa de los Balcones** – or, to give it its Sunday-best name, Casa Mendez-Fonseca. It's best known for its splendid, ornately worked Canarian pine balconies

facing both onto the street and into its delightful courtyard. The ground floor contains a lace and linen centre, while the upper level has a small **museum** showing the house as it would have been in the eighteenth century.

Iglesia de la Concepción

MAP P.54

Plaza Casañas, La Orotava ⓦ concepcionorotava.com. Mon–Fri 10.30am–1pm; mass Mon–Sat 7.30pm, Sun 10am & noon.

Built after the original church on this site was destroyed by earthquakes in 1704 and 1705, **Iglesia de la Concepción** is considered the finest example of Baroque architecture in the Canary Islands. The elaborate dome is best viewed from inside, alongside the Neoclassical Genovese tabernacle.

Iglesia de San Agustín

MAP P.54

C/San Agustín 2, La Orotava ☎ 922 32 69 24. Mon–Fri 10am–1pm; Mass Sun 6pm.

Dating from the second half of the seventeenth century, **Iglesia de San Agustín** was built for the Augustinian Order and financed by the twelve most powerful families in the valley, the owners of the Doce Casas. As the town was exclusively under the control of the Dominicans at the time, this was a show of power, wealth and influence by the families. The north wall is one of the most beautiful facades in the Canary Islands and is distinct for its four Roman arches. Presiding over the altar is the seventeenth-century figure of Nuestra Señora de Gracia by Portuguese sculptor Manuel Pareira.

Jardín Marquesado de la Quinta Roja and Jardínes Botánicos

MAP P.54

Plaza de la Constitución 7, La Orotava. Mon–Fri 9am–8pm, Sat & Sun 9.30am–8.30pm. Free.

When the Catholic Church refused to allow the body of the Eighth Marquis of Quinta Roja to be interred in sacred ground because he was a Freemason, his mother commissioned the marble mausoleum which sits at the top of the Italianate gardens of **Jardín Marquesado de la Quinta Roja** (also called Victoria Gardens). Here, her son's final resting place would be in full view of the whole town, as a snub to the church. Just west of here, behind the *ayuntamiento*, are La Orotava's own tiny **Jardínes Botánicos** (same hours), which include a good-sized dragon tree amid a small collection of exotic plants.

Molino La Máquina

Molino La Máquina

MAP P.54

C/Colegio 3, La Orotava ☎ 922 33 07 03. Mon–Thu 8.30am––6pm, Fri 8.30am–3pm, Sat 8am–3pm. Free.

El Farrobo, the town's old mill quarter, is where the local speciality **gofio** (see page 142) has been produced for centuries. Nowadays, seven of the original *gofio* mills still survive along the phenomenally steep Calle de San Francisco, and one of them, **Molino La Máquina**, still operates, albeit now with an electric motor, and has a regular supply of local customers. Photos inside depict bygone days when the quarter still clattered with the sound of the mills. Try one of their *gofio* energy bars for a mid-morning boost.

Arrival and information

La Orotava's **bus station** is just off Avenida Obispo Benítez de Lugo. The #345 and #353 connect the town with nearby Puerto de la Cruz (35 daily; 18min). There are also regular buses to Santa Cruz and Isla Baja in the west. It's a five-minute walk west to the **tourist office** (Mon–Fri 8am–6pm, Sat & Sun 9am–1pm; ☎ 922 32 30 41) on Calle Cantos Canarios 1 at the start of the old town.

Casa del Vino la Baranda

Museo de Artesanía Iberoamericana

MAP P.54

C/Tomás Zerolo 34, La Orotava
Ⓦ artenerife.com/museo-de-artesania.
Mon–Fri 10am–3pm, Sat 10am–2pm. Free.
Housed in the splendid
former Convento de Santo
Domingo, **Museo de Artesanía
Iberoamericana** exhibits handicrafts
and folk art from Spain and Latin
America. Its extensive collection
includes fascinating pieces such as a
guitar made from an armadillo, and
depictions of Los Muertos. Displays

are labelled in English as well as
Spanish, French and German.

El Sauzal

MAP P.50

Bus #101 and #104 from Puerto de la Cruz
or Santa Cruz, every 30min, 40min.
In the nineteenth-century **El Sauzal**
was the last stop on the stagecoach
which took explorers and scientists
to Parque Nacional del Teide. Today
its treasures lie far beneath the
tourist radar. The town's Carretera
General del Norte plays host to
a plethora of good restaurants,
including Tacoa which brews its
own ales on the premises, while the
eclectic **Parque de los Lavaderos**
which tumbles down the cliffside
has stunning views along the
northwest coast to Mount Teide.

Casa del Vino la Baranda

MAP P.50

C/San Simón 49, El Sauzal; buses #101 and
#104 from Puerto de la Cruz or Santa Cruz,
every 30min, 40min Ⓦ casadelvinotenerife.
com. Tues–Sat 10am–8pm, Sun 10am–6pm.
Free.
Tenerife's wine museum is housed in
a beautifully restored seventeenth-
century *hacienda*. Informative
displays give details on the
development of the island's wine
trade and a **tasting room** enables
you to try before you buy. The tapas
bar and restaurant has excellent
views over the coast.

Corpus Christi Flower Carpets

In 1847 Lady Leanor del Castillo decided to create a **carpet of flowers**
outside her gate for the Corpus Christi procession to walk across.
The tradition caught on, and today at **Corpus Christi** (May/June)
the streets surrounding the Iglesia de la Concepción are carpeted
in elaborate designs constructed entirely from flower petals, seeds
and grasses. In the plaza fronting the *ayuntamiento* (town hall), an
intricate, biblical illustration is created by skilled *alfombristas* (carpet
makers) exclusively from soil collected in Parque Nacional del Teide.
Go to a balcony on the first floor of the *ayuntamiento* for the best view.
At the end of the day, the church procession walks right through these
exquisite, transient works of art, destroying them in the process.
Incidentally, the Castillo family still creates a carpet outside their gate,
over a century and a half later.

Shops

Artenerife

MAP P.50

Casa de la Aduana, Puerto de la Cruz
📞 922 33 40 13, 🌐 artenerife.com. Daily
10am–8pm.

Pottery, lace, jewellery and carvings
are some of the genuine Tenerife
souvenirs available at this branch of
the island-wide chain.

Casa Lercaro

MAP P.54

C/Colegio 7, La Orotava 🌐 casalercaro.com.
Daily 8.30am–7pm.

Avoid the crowds at Casa Turistica,
the one of the Doce Casas to which
tour groups are taken, and head
instead to the lovely Casa Lercaro;
the ground floor and courtyard
house a delightful restaurant,
while the upper floor is home to
a shop crammed with ornaments,
trinkets, antiques and collectibles.
You'll find inlaid jewellery boxes,
hand-painted fans, decorative wine
glass covers and in season, beautiful
Christmas ornaments.

La Ranilla Espacio Artesano

MAP P.50

C/Mequinez 59, Puerto de la Cruz
🌐 laranilla.org. Mon–Fri 10am–2pm &
5–8pm, Sat 10am–2pm.

Retail outlet for a small collective
of artisans selling an interesting
selection of bags, jewellery,
ornaments and artwork. They all
make great gifts and souvenirs.

Café

Ébano Cafe

MAP P.50

C/Hoya 2, Puerto de la Cruz 📞 922 38 86
32. Daily 10am–10pm.

Cakes, coffee and views of Plaza
de la Iglesia at the Art Deco-styled
Ébano, the most elegant spot in
town to while away the afternoon
people-watching.

Restaurants

Bistro de Antonio Aguiar

MAP P.50

C/Pérez Zamora 12, Puerto de la Cruz
📞 646 06 11 72. Wed 6–10.30pm, Thu–Sun
1–4pm & 7–10.30pm.

The direct manner of renowned local
chef Antonio Aguiar might not be
to everyone's taste, but his classic
Canarian food should be. He cooks a
mean *conejo*, a speciality of the house
being rabbit with chestnuts and sweet
potato. £

Bodega Julian

MAP P.50

C/Mequinez 20, Perto de la Cruz 📞 686 55
63 15. Tue–Thu 6–11pm, Fri & Sat 1–4pm
& 6–11pm.

A handful of Spanish dishes are
served with soulful ballads courtesy
of Julian and his waiting staff. It
might sound tacky, but the singing
serving staff deliver a surprisingly
emotional experience and the food
is good, especially the lamb. £

Casa Lercaro

MAP P.54

C/Colegio 7, La Orotava 🌐 casalercaro.com.
Thu–Sat 10am–10pm, Sun 11am–7pm.

Located in the exquisite interior
courtyard of one of La Orotava's
most elegant colonial mansions,
with panoramic views across the
valley to Puerto de la Cruz. This
is the sort of place in which you
could easily lose an afternoon,
sipping local wine while picking at
platters of local cheese and *jamón
Ibérico*. £

Casa Mediterránea

MAP P.50

C/Benjamin J Miranda 5, Puerto de la Cruz
📞 922 38 27 11. Wed–Sat 1–3.30pm &
6.30–10pm, Sun 1–3.30pm & 6.30–9.30pm.

Bijou, Argentine-owned restaurant
with a handful of tables outside.
Steak is the popular choice from
the main menu, while *empanada
Argentina* and *queso provolone* are
the tapas menu showstoppers. £

El Taller Seve Diaz

El Taller Seve Diaz

MAP P.50

C/San Felipe 32, Puerto de la Cruz ⓦ eltallersevediaz.com. Wed–Fri 7–11pm, Sat & Sun 1–3pm & 7–11pm.

Creative Canarian cuisine from the kitchen of one of the new breed of talented young *tinerfeño* chefs. Traditional dishes are perked up to satisfy twenty-first century palates: gazpacho can feature raspberry, for instance, while a local favourite fish, *cherne*, is served as ravioli. The daily tasting menu is a special treat. £–££

Haydee

MAP P.54

Barranco La Arena 53, Dehesa Baja, 38300 La Orotava ⓦ restaurantehaydee.rest. Thurs & Fri 7.30–10.30pm, Sat 1.30–4pm & 7–10.30pm, Sun 10am–4pm.

Chef patron Víctor Suárez trained with the famous Adriá brothers, so expect something special from this restaurant. Dining rooms set in traditional *casitas* with a terrace overlooking banana plantations and a Canarian/Asian fusion menu set *Haydee* apart from the crowd. The menu changes regularly, but a constant is *cochino negro* (black pig) in a bao bun; the *jamón Ibérico* is also delicious. £££ (tasting menu ££££)

Tasca El Olivo

MAP P.50

C/Iriarte 1, Puerto de la Cruz ⓦ tascaelolivo. eatbu.com. Wed & Thurs 1–10pm, Fri & Sat 1–10.30pm, Sun 1–3.30pm.

Good quality Spanish tapas and main courses in a friendly *tasca* located on a quiet back street. The *pulpito al Olivo* is a revelation, showing that octopus and mashed potato are truly made for each other. £

Tasca Ihuey

MAP P.50

C/San Felipe 34, Puerto de la Cruz ⓦ ihueytasca.es. Wed–Fri 6–10.30pm, Sat & Sun 1.30–10pm.

One of a trio of tasty restaurants on the same street, all serving food that dares to be different from the traditional menus found in many

La Duquesa

MAP P.54

Plaza Patricio García 6, La Orotava ☎ 922 33 49 49. Mon–Fri 7am–4pm.

Good lunch venue in a traditional cottage beside the Iglesia de la Concepción and the statue of the *alfombrista* (carpet maker). Inside it's quaint and cosy, while the wooden terrace fills quickly. The menu features traditional Canarian dishes such as *ropa vieja*, a sort of leftovers slow-cooked stew whose English translation is "old clothes". £

El Limón

MAP P.50

C/Esquivel 4, Puerto de la Cruz ☎ 922 38 16 19. Daily noon–10pm, closed Wed.

Popular with local and visiting vegetarians, fresh and zesty *El Limón* has been serving meat-free tapas, burgers and salads for a couple of decades. Vegetarian options are increasingly popular as a refreshing change on an island where most meals revolve around meat. Burgers and main courses like seitan fillet with spinach tortilla and salad are reasonably priced and full of flavour. £

restaurants around the town. Prawn ravioli is intriguing and their white chocolate soup dessert is genius. £ (tasting menu ££)

Terraza del Sauzal

MAP P.50

Pasaje Sierve de Dios 9, El Sauzal Ⓦ terrazasdelsauzal.com. Wed–Fri 1–10.30pm, Sat & Sun 10am–10.30pm.

The menu features a stylish fusion of Canarian and international dishes, the location is inside the grounds of a colonial finca, and the views of Mount Teide and Tenerife's north coast are superb. What's not to like? Ideal for lunch, but the special Terraza cava brunch is even better (only available Sat & Sun 10–11.30am). £

Tito's Bodeguita

MAP P.50

C/del Durazno 1, Puerto de la Cruz Ⓦ titosbodeguita.com. Mon–Sat 12.30–11pm.

Located on the outskirts of town, *Tito's* is set inside a charming seventeenth-century colonial mansion and is a popular lunch venue. Small menu with Spanish/ Canarian influences, try the *caprichos de pollo*, crispy chicken strips in an almond sauce. £

Tito's Bodeguita

Bars and clubs

Agora Bar & Café

MAP P.50

Plaza Benito Perez Galdos 6, Puerto de la Cruz 634 35 13 60. Mon 3.30–11.30pm, Tue–Thu 11am–midnight, Fri 11am–1am, Sat 10am–1am, Sun 10am–midnight.

Lively spot where anything goes, from language exchanges to art classes in the afternoon, followed by an eclectic roster of live music and dancing in the evening. Food and bottled beers from independent breweries available. £

Blanco Bar

MAP P.50

C/Blanco 12, Puerto de la Cruz Ⓦ blancobar.com. Sun–Thurs 8pm–3am, Fri & Sat 9pm–5am. Entry fee varies.

Blanco is part cocktail bar, part live music venue part comedy club, depending on what's on. Entry fees vary: at peak times it's €5 (one drink included), but if there's a fairly well-known band (in Spanish music circles) playing, it may be €10. Check the website for events. Weekends after midnight are liveliest. £

Garachico and the Teno

Centre of the Isla Baja region, which includes Buenavista del Norte, Los Silos and Masca, Garachico is considered Tenerife's most picturesque town, its cobbled streets and handsome plazas welcoming day-trippers in their hordes. Once the tour coaches depart, Garachico reverts to its usual tranquil self, with its boutique hotels providing an excellent base for exploring Icod de los Vinos, the Isla Baja region and the excellent hiking in spectacular Parque Nacional del Teno.

El Caletón rock pools

MAP P.61

Avda República de Venezuela

One of Garachico's unique attractions is a series of **rock pools** alongside the Castillo de San Miguel. Honed from solidified lava which cooled on contact with the sea, these are fed and cleaned by the tidal action. The pools, which are of varying depth and are good to explore as many are teeming with tropical fish, are hugely popular with local youths on summer weekends. High spring and autumn tides can put them temporarily out of bounds.

Castillo de San Miguel

MAP P.61

Avda Tomé Cano ⊕ 922 83 00 00. Mon–Sat 10am–4pm. €3.

The stocky, harbourside fort of **Castillo de San Miguel** was built in the sixteenth-century to protect Garachico from pirates. One of the few buildings to survive the 1706 volcanic eruption, it's now home to a small **museum** (ask for the English text for displays). There are good views from the ramparts

El Caletón

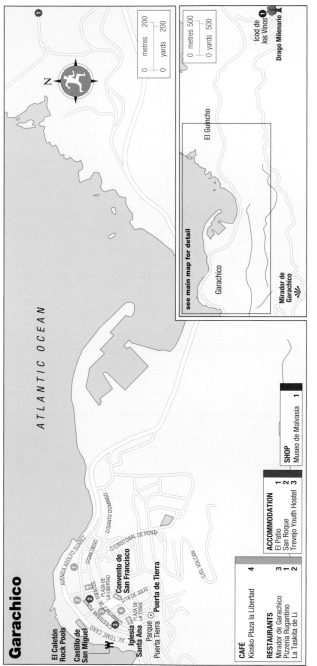

Garachico

ATLANTIC OCEAN

El Caletón Rock Pools
Castillo de San Miguel
Convento de San Francisco
Iglesia Santa Ana
Parque Puerta Tierra · **Puerta de Tierra**

AVENIDA ADOLFO SUÁREZ
C/SAN DIEGO
C/SANTO DOMINGO
C/CRISTÓBAL DE PONTE
C/ESTEBAN DE PONTE
C/SAN TOMÉ CANO
PLAZA DE LA LIBERTAD
C/18 DE JULIO
PLAZA DE SANTA ANA
AV. TOMÉ CANO
CI/EL VOLCÁN

CAFÉ
Kiosko Plaza la Libertad ... 4

RESTAURANTS
Mirador de Garachico ... 3
Pizzeria Rugantino ... 1
La Taskita de Li ... 2

ACCOMMODATION
El Patio ... 1
San Roque ... 2
Trevejo Youth Hostel ... 3

SHOP
Museo de Malvasia ... 1

N

0 metres 200
0 yards 200

0 metres 500
0 yards 500

see main map for detail

El Guincho
Garachico
Mirador de Garachico

Icod de los Vinos
Drago Milenario

The volcanic eruption of 1706

During the sixteenth century, Garachico grew immeasurably rich on **trade** between Europe and the New World, its natural harbour providing safe berth for merchant ships. Attracted by the trade opportunities, the rich and powerful of Europe built elaborate mansions in the town and, where the money was, the clergy soon followed. But all that changed on the morning of May 5, 1706, when Montaña Negra **erupted** and sent two columns of lava flowing down the cliffs towards Garachico. By nightfall, 384 neighbourhoods and the harbour had been engulfed and destroyed. With its harbour gone, the focus of trading shifted first to Puerto de la Cruz and then to Santa Cruz, leaving Garachico to begin the laborious job of rebuilding.

across the village and out to the Roque de Garachico, a lone rock monolith in the bay.

Plaza de la Libertad

MAP P.61

The town's main square, located two streets behind Avenida República de Venezuela, **Plaza de la Libertad** is arguably Tenerife's most striking, with its sixteenth-century, Moorish styled Iglesia de Nuestra Señora de los Ángeles flanked by the former Convento de San Francisco and the Neoclassical town hall. Finishing off this bevvy of beauties is the terracotta face of the Quinta Roja with its carved

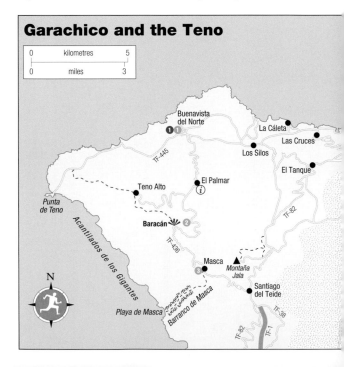

Garachico and the Teno

wooden balconies. On the western end of the plaza stands the grand Iglesia Santa Ana, the town's main church, topped by a six-storey belltower and containing a fine wooden ceiling.

Parque Puerta Tierra

MAP P.61

Narrow Calle Esteban Ponte divides rows of elegant town houses as it runs through the centre of Garachico to **Parque Puerta Tierra**. A small park in the square with an old wine press and a Poet's Corner, pride of place goes to the only thing left of the harbour following the 1706 eruption, La Puerta de Tierra (the toll gate).

Buenavista del Norte

MAP P.62

Buses #107 from Santa Cruz, 4–6 daily, 1hr 35min; #363 from Puerto de la Cruz, 16–25 daily, 1hr 15min; and #363 from Garachico, 16–25 daily, 15min.

Tucked into the northwest corner of the island at the foot of the sheer sides of the Teno massif, **Buenavista del Norte** is one of the island's oldest towns, settlers having been drawn here by its beauty and its fertile soil. Growing prosperous on sugar cane, sadly the forests were destroyed to provide fuel for its refineries. Today the town has a strong agricultural heritage, a pretty coastal walk and a lovely old quarter, largely ignored by those en route to the golf course. Visit during **San Abad** (around Jan 15) and enjoy one of the largest livestock fairs on Tenerife.

Punta de Teno

MAP P.62

Bus #369 hourly Sat, Sun & fiestas 10am–5pm from Buenavista bus station.

Drive beyond Buenavista and you'll be met by enormous, fear-inducing boards telling you

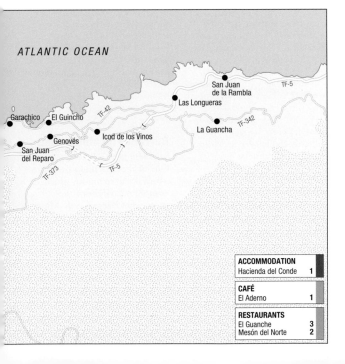

ATLANTIC OCEAN

Garachico · El Guincho · Genovés · San Juan del Reparo · Icod de los Vinos · Las Longueras · San Juan de la Rambla · La Guancha · TF-5 · TF-42 · TF-342 · TF-373

ACCOMMODATION	
Hacienda del Conde	1

CAFÉ	
El Aderno	1

RESTAURANTS	
El Guanche	3
Mesón del Norte	2

Punta de Teno lighthouse

not to pass if it's wet or windy. A sinuous road tunnel follows the contours of **Punta de Teno**, suspended between the rock face and the ocean. A bridge between microclimates, you can enter beneath leaden skies and emerge into unbroken blue at what feels like the edge of the world. There you'll find an old lighthouse, a sheltered bay with fine views over to Los Gigantes, and superb sunsets over La Gomera and La Palma. At weekends and on fiesta days cars are not permitted, and only the bus ferries visitors through the tunnel.

Los Silos

MAP P.62

Bus #363: 26 daily from Puerto de la Cruz, 1hr 10min; 26 daily from Buenavista, 40min.

A pretty little town, **Los Silos**' streets are too narrow for tour buses which means that, while Garachico entertains the day-trippers, neighbouring Los Silos remains gloriously crowd-free. An Art Nouveau plaza and bandstand lie at the heart of the town, surrounded by traditional houses spanning back four centuries. Favoured by neo-hippies and German residents who have restored its historic houses, the town holds an annual storytelling festival in early December. Its coastal development of El Puertito displays a full-sized whale skeleton alongside a swimming pool complex.

Masca

MAP P.62

Bus #355: 4 daily from Buenavista, 25min; 4 daily from Santiago del Teide, 30min.

Taking the prize for Tenerife's most spectacular setting, the village of **Masca** balances along the crease of two gorges in the Teno mountain range, flanked on three sides by jagged pinnacles and looking out over the Atlantic to La Gomera. The white-knuckle drive that connects it to Santiago del Teide and Buenavista was only constructed in the 1970s and is not for the faint-hearted driver. Steep, cobbled paths call for sensible footwear and lead to the bottom of the village, from where the views back over Teno are hypnotic. After the Parque Nacional del Teide, this is Tenerife's most popular day-trip destination. Avoid the worst of the crowds by visiting before 10am, after 5pm and on Fridays.

Barranco de Masca hike

MAP P.62

One of the best **hikes** on the island is the strenuous, three-hour, 8km trek down the steep-sided **Barranco de Masca**, beginning near the bottom of the village and traversing the ravine to reach a small beach, where a boat picks hikers up and ferries them to Los Gigantes (buy tickets in the village before setting off). Those who have the stamina may choose to hike their way back up to Masca village rather than have the expense of a taxi back from Los Gigantes to collect their car (around €25). A stunning hike through an almost prehistoric landscape, this is no walk in the park and many people have gravely underestimated its difficulty, resulting in numerous accidents and deaths. Consequently, the area was closed for three years until it reopened in 2021 under a new pilot programme that greatly restricts the number of people that can book and enter the gorge at one time. Several companies offer hiking trips down the valley, collecting from the main coastal resorts, and it is recommended to join one rather than going alone.

Icod de los Vinos

MAP P.62
Buses #363 from Puerto de la Cruz, 26 daily, 45min; #325 from Los Gigantes, 6 daily, 35min; #363 from Garachico, 16–25 daily, 10min.

Known primarily for its Drago Milenario (see page 66), **Icod de los Vinos** has more to offer than just its tree – good shopping, the sixteenth-century Iglesia de San Marcos and the pretty Plaza Pila surrounded by sixteenth-, seventeenth- and eighteenth-century balconied houses to name a few attractions. Plaza Pila is also where you'll find the little Malvasia Museum (see page 67) dedicated to the sweet wine that was Shakespeare's favourite tipple. Those who want to view the famous Drago Milenario without paying to wander through the botanics garden can get a fine view from Plaza de San Marcos.

Parque del Drago

MAP P.62
Paseo Nicolas Estevez Borges 7 ☎ 922 81 22 26. Fri–Tue 8am–6pm, Wed 9am–3pm, Thu 10am–6pm. €5.

Parque del Drago contains the most famous of the Dragon Tree survivors, the so-called **Drago Milenario** which, despite its nomenclature, is believed to be in the region of 800 years old. This magnificent specimen is over 16m tall and its circumference is 20m at the base, making it not only the oldest but the largest Dragon Tree in the archipelago. Now shored up against the

Drago Milenario, Icod de Los Vinos

Drago Milenario – The Dragon Tree

Once common around the Mediterranean, successive ice ages pushed the **dragon tree** (*dracaena draco*) further south around twenty million years ago, restricting its habitat to the Macronesian Islands. Guanche elders and kings held court beneath its canopy and believed the tree foretold the future, a full blossom promising a fine harvest. The tree's sap is known as **dragon's blood** as it oxidises red on contact with air. The Guanches used the sap in their mummification process but its uses elsewhere were manifold. Venetian noblewomen used it to dye their hair, Florentine masons tinted marble with it and master violin makers added it to varnish for extra resonance. Demand for the sap meant that many trees were tapped to death, and today there are few large specimens left.

effects of vibration from the nearby roads, the tree stands in its own park, which contains an impressive collection of endemic flora.

Teno Alto

MAP P.62
Bus #355 #365 or #366 from Buenavista to El Palmar; 16 daily; 10–15min.

The small hamlet of **Teno Alto** sits on the cusp of microclimate zones atop the northwest corner of the island. A beautiful trail leads from Los Pedragales in El Palmar and climbs to Los Bailaderos in Teno Alto. From there, a further path takes you along the ridge to Baracan with expansive views across Teno – and if it's a clear day, one of the best views of Teide on the whole island – before descending back into El Palmar. In spring, this route is splendid when awash with wild flowers.

Teno Alto

Shop

Museo de Malvasia

Plaza de la Pila 5, Icod de los Vinos
Ⓦ museomalvasia.com. Tue–Sat 11am–6pm.
Wonderful museum and shop
dedicated to the fruit of the vine,
Malvasia, and its myriad wine-
quaffing wordsmiths; most notably,
the Bard himself. You can taste and
buy Canarian wines and liqueurs or
sign up for a class on how to make
local specialities such as *mojo*.

Cafés

El Aderno

C/Alhóndiga 8, Buenavista del Norte
Ⓦ eladerno.com. Mon–Sat 9am–8pm, Sun
8am–8pm.
This is the original *El Aderno*, whose
artisan cakes and chocolates are
allegedly enjoyed by Spanish royalty.
There is a small amount of seating
in the shop. Cakes from €2.

Kiosko Plaza la Libertad

C/Francisco Montesdeoca y García
1, Garachico ☏ 661 00 24 33. Daily
10am–10pm.
While visitors favour the café at El
Caletón rock pools, *Kiosko Plaza
de la Libertad* is where you'll find
the locals socialising and drinking
cortados or *barraquitos* in the shade
of Indian bay trees.

Restaurants

El Guanche

C/El Lomito, Masca Ⓦ elguanchealteschule.
es. Thu–Mon noon–5pm.
This former rural schoolhouse is
not only in a stunning location, it
has a surprising menu – vegetarian
dishes made with local produce.
Try the platter of local cheeses with
a glass of cactus juice. £

Mesón del Norte

C/Masca 1, Las Portelas, Buenavista del
Norte Ⓦ restaurantemesondelnorte.es. Sun
& Tue–Thu noon–5pm, Fri & Sat noon–5pm
& 6.30–10.30pm.
Rural restaurant, 6km south of
Buenavista on the road to Masca,
offering inexpensive, good-quality
Canarian cuisine, especially grilled
meats, along with fresh goat's cheese
and local wines including their
own. The *menú del día* is very good
value. £

Mirador de Garachico

C/Francisco Martínez de Fuentes 17,
Garachico Ⓦ miradordegarachico.com.
Fri–Tue 1–10.30pm.
Despite the name, there are
no views here, just good food
creatively presented and friendly,
efficient service. Occasional theme
weeks include such fancies as
'flower cuisine'. There is also a
small shop selling fresh produce.
£–££

Pizzería Rugantino

C/Esteban de Ponte 47, Garachico ☏ 634
35 11 71. Fri & Sat 7pm–midnight, Sun
6pm–midnight.
A pizzeria which is so good it only
needs to open at weekends and so
popular that locals queue to get
in. Even visiting Michelin-starred
chefs have been known to eat here.
Getting there early or reserving a
table is essential. Still reasonably
priced. £

La Taskita de Li

C. Esteban de Ponte 35, Garachico, ☏ 648
48 25 76. Sun–Fri noon–4pm & 6.30–10pm.
Small family-run restaurant, expect
service to be slow at busy times, but
staff are pleasant and you may be
lucky enough to have someone play
the piano while you dine. A limited
selection of wines and a changing
dessert menu, but everything is
fresh and home-cooked. £

The west coast

The sunniest part of Tenerife, the west coast comprises a string of resorts stretching from the magnificent Acantilados de Los Gigantes (cliffs of the giants) in the northwest corner to the developments of Costa Adeje in the southwest. Chief among them is Los Gigantes, whose location never ceases to induce gasps from first time visitors. Joined at its hip are the quieter Puerto de Santiago and Playa de la Arena, largely family-oriented resorts offering a more low-key alternative to Playa de Las Américas. Moving south, the workaday roadside shops of Alcalá and Playa de San Juan mask pretty coastal developments and a more authentic *tinerfeño* feel, while in the hills above the coast, Santiago del Teide epitomises traditional rural Tenerife.

Los Gigantes

MAP P.69

Crammed into every inch of available space between its eponymous cliffs and its marina, **Los Gigantes** mainly consists of a jumble of low-rise holiday and housing developments spilling down the cliffside. Built by UK nationals in the 1960s, its feel remains singularly British and it even manages to exude a vaguely village atmosphere. By day, most life bustles around the marina which is lined with restaurants and from where multiple boat and whale-watching excursions set sail. After dark, it's the restaurants and bars lining the main street and around the plaza that attract the most visitors.

Mirador Archipenque

MAP P.69

Carretera General, Puerto de Santiago, Acantilados de Los Gigantes.

Not easy to reach by public transport, but worth a stop off if you are driving or hiking nearby. The mirador is well signposted off the main road and there is a small coffee shop where you can sit and enjoy a drink and snack, with a few souvenirs on sale too (☎922 86 29 51. Tue–Sun 10am–6pm). Catching the view across the cliffs at sundown can be stuning.

Puerto de Santiago and Playa de la Arena

MAP P.69

What **Puerto de Santiago** lacks in looks, it makes up for in authentic

Arrival and information

The #325 **bus** runs between Los Gigantes, Puerto de Santiago and Playa de la Arena and Puerto de la Cruz (6 daily; 1hr 45min). The #473 and #477 also connect them, via Alcalá and Playa San Juan, with Costa Adeje and Los Cristianos (27 daily; 1hr 5min–1hr 20min), where travellers can change to routes covering a wider range of destinations. There are **tourist offices** in Los Gigantes (Av Jose Gonzalez Forte 10 ☎922 86 81 86; Tues–Sat 8am–4pm) and Playa San Juan (Av Juan Carlos 1 ☎922 13 89 87; Mon–Fri 9am–3pm).

Puerto de Santiago

character. A diminutive beach in a sheltered bay and a row of fish and seafood restaurants characterise the fishing harbour, while touristy developments cluster around the *Barcelo Santiago* hotel. By contrast,

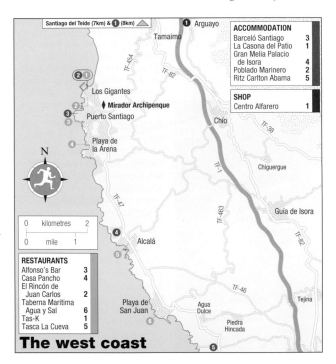

Santiago del Teide (7km) & ① (8km) ▲

① Arguayo

Tamaimo

TF-454

TF-82

② ①

Los Gigantes

♦ Mirador Archipenque

② ③

Puerto Santiago

Chío

TF-38

④ Playa de la Arena

Chiguergue

N

TF-1

TF-47

TF-463

Guía de Isora

TF-82

0 kilometres 2

0 mile 1

④ Alcalá

⑤

TF-46

Tejina

RESTAURANTS

Alfonso's Bar	3
Casa Pancho	4
El Rincón de Juan Carlos	2
Taberna Maritima Agua y Sal	6
Tas-K	1
Tasca La Cueva	5

Playa de San Juan

Agua Dulce

⑥

Piedra Hincada

The west coast

⑤

ACCOMMODATION

Barceló Santiago	3
La Casona del Patio	1
Gran Melia Palacio de Isora	4
Poblado Marinero	2
Ritz Carlton Abama	5

SHOP

Centro Alfarero	1

Whale- and dolphin-watching

The waters between Los Gigantes and La Gomera are deep and warm, attracting a host of microscopic marine life which in turn, supports twenty-eight species of resident and migratory cetaceans, including pods of **bottle-nosed dolphins** and schools of **pilot whales**. Multiple daily excursions from Los Gigantes marina typically cost €15–€35 for two hours and include a visit to Masca bay and to the Los Gigantes cliffs. Make sure the boat is flying the yellow *barco azul* flag which indicates it's complying with international guidelines to protect the cetaceans. Trips like Flipper Uno and Nashira Uno provide food, booze and a chance to swim in Masca bay. For a more authentic experience, choose the Katrin. Whale- and dolphin-watching excursions also depart regularly from Los Cristianos and from Puerto Colón in Playa de Las Américas (see page 73).

neighbouring **Playa de la Arena** is a family resort which lacks Canarian character but has a gently shelving beach that frames the island of La Gomera between its headlands.

Alcalá
MAP P.69

Descend towards the coast from **Alcalá**'s perpetually busy road and you'll find a lovely plaza surrounded by restaurants and cafés and leading to a miniscule beach, with

Bottle-nosed dolphin

extensive sun terraces atop the cliffs. Retaining its authenticity despite the luxury hotel on its doorstep, visit around August 15 for the distinctly Latin American **fiestas** and spectacular fireworks.

Playa de San Juan
MAP P.69

Playa de San Juan retains its Canarian character, but feels somewhat more upmarket than Alcalá. The main attractions are its long beach backed by restaurant terraces, its pretty marina and its sunset views over La Gomera.

Santiago del Teide
MAP P.69

Bus #325 from Los Gigantes, 6 daily, 8min; #460 from Costa Adeje taking in all the west coast resorts, 8 daily, 1hr.

The contrast between the coastal resorts and the municipal capital of **Santiago del Teide** could not be more marked. A picturesque one-horse hill town set in the Valle de Santiago, a handful of whitewashed houses, restaurants and cafés straddles the road. Highlights are the Iglesia de San Fernando Rey and the seventeenth-century Casa del Patio. A lovely **hike** begins from Valle de Arriba and climbs along an almond-blossom trail (blooming from late Jan/Feb) to Montaña Bilma.

Shop

Centro Alfarero

MAP P.69

Arguayo ☎ 922 86 34 65. Tues–Sun 10am–1pm & 4–7pm.

For the chance to watch rough-hewn traditional pots being made using thousand-year-old Guanche techniques, this is the place to come. The small shop sells the finished goods. Driving is the only practical way to get here.

Restaurants

Alfonso's Bar

MAP P.69

Carretera General 28, Puerto de Santiago ☎ 922 86 23 34. Daily 9.30am–11pm.

Unassuming bar/restaurant above Puerto de Santiago's beach. The menu promises tapas and typical local food and that's exactly what *Alfonso's Bar* delivers, including *carne de cabra* (goat) and grilled *dorada* (bream). £.

Casa Pancho

MAP P.69

Av Marítima, Playa de la Arena ⓦ restaurantepancho.es. Tues–Sat 1–4pm & 8–10pm, Sun 1–4pm.

A quality Canarian restaurant in a superb location on the beach almost as popular with Spanish diners as with British. Appealing to both is the house speciality, *paella*. Slightly more expensive than other restaurants in the area, but still very reasonable. £

El Rincón de Juan Carlos

MAP P.69

Paisaje Jacaranda 2, Los Gigantes ⓦ elrincondejuancarlos.com. Tues–Sat 7–10pm.

Possibly the best restaurant in the Canary Islands, *El Rincón de Juan Carlos* might have a Michelin star but it's still a friendly, family-run affair. The tasting menu isn't cheap, but it represents good value for such outstanding quality. ££££

El Rincón de Juan Carlos

Taberna Marítima Agua y Sal

MAP P.69

Playa San Juan ☎ 922 08 57 68. Tues–Sat 12.30–10.30pm, Sun 12.30–4.30pm.

Fresh fish and seafood, right on the seafront. A huge selection, which can be served with pasta or rice and various sauces, but the star of the show is the simple pan-fried fish. £

Tas-K

MAP P.69

C/los Guíos 16, Los Gigantes ☎ 922 186 23 28. Tues–Sat noon–11pm.

A breath of fresh air in a resort which overwhelmingly caters for British visitors, *Tas-K* has a decent tapas menu featuring Spanish classics such as *jamón Iberico* as well as some Canarian favourites like *almogrote*, a strong cheese pâté from La Gomera. £

Tasca La Cueva

MAP P.69

C/la Plaza 22, Alcalá ☎ 609 46 68 88. Daily 6.30–11.30pm (closed Tue).

Enjoy a platter of local cheeses and *pimientos de Padrón* on the terraza or inside at a barrel table. Portions are generous. £–££

The southwest resorts

Tenerife's number one holiday hotspot, the resorts of Los Cristianos, Playa de Las Américas and Costa Adeje sprawl seamlessly ever further west from the southern tip of the island, engulfing everything in their path. Costa Adeje, just a decade ago little more than an idea jotted on a marketer's notepad, now spreads so far northwest that anyone booking a holiday in its outer limit of Callao Salvaje will find themselves a forty-minute bus ride away from the main resort area, while new resorts continue to open and expand the area. A holiday pleasure dome with beaches, theme parks, luxurious hotels and almost guaranteed sunshine, the appeal of the southwestern coastal resorts seems insatiable. If it's authentic *tinerfeño* culture you're looking for, though, then other than a small pocket around the harbour of Los Cristianos you'll have to head inland to Adeje to find it.

Los Cristianos

MAP P.74

Originally no more than a harbour and a few fishing huts dotted along the shore, **Los Cristianos** experienced exponential growth in the 1950s when a Swedish broadcaster and multiple sclerosis sufferer found that the climate sent his disease into remission. Still the island's most disability-friendly resort, it now attracts a more mature visitor, one who prefers to give the lively nightlife of its Playa de Las Américas neighbour a wide berth. As the gateway to the islands of La Gomera, La Palma and El Hierro, alongside the pleasure cruises, regular ferries depart from the harbour, one of the few places in the resort that still retains a traditional feel.

Playa de las Vistas

MAP P.74

The vast stretch of golden sand that fringes the coastline of Los Cristianos beyond the port and stretches all the way to Las Américas, **Playa de las Vistas** is the beach of choice for many visitors to the south. Regimented rows of sun loungers occupy the middle ground, still leaving long stretches of hot sand to negotiate en route to the sea where a gently shelving shoreline makes it very popular with families. Behind the beach, endless bars, restaurants, ice cream parlours and souvenir shops line the promenade.

Ferries to the western Canary Islands

Regular daily **ferries** connect Los Cristianos to the islands of La Gomera, La Palma and El Hierro and show visitors an entirely different face to the Canary Islands. Ferries are operated by Fred Olsen (La Gomera and La Palma; ⊛ fredolsen.es) and Naviera Armas (La Gomera, La Palma and El Hierro; ⊛ navieraarmas.com).

Arrival and information

Frequent **buses** (#451 every 30min, #450 hourly) depart from the South airport for Los Cristianos and Las Américas, terminating at the bus station in Costa Adeje. There are **tourist offices** in Los Cristianos, on Plaza Pescador (Mon–Fri 9am–4.30pm; ☎ 922 75 71 30) and on Playa las Vistas (daily 9am–4.30pm, ☎ 922 78 70 11); in Playa de Las Américas on Avenida Rafael Puig Lluvina 19, opposite Parque Santiago II (Mon–Sat 9am–4.30pm, ☎ 922 79 76 68); and in Costa Adeje alongside Playa de Troya (daily 10am–5pm, ☎ 922 98 50 80) and Playa Fañabé (daily 10am–5pm, ☎ 922 71 65 39).

Playa de Las Américas

MAP P.74

Casting off its "Brits behaving badly" hangover of the 1990s, very little is left of the **Playa de Las Américas** that achieved holiday hell notoriety. Massive investment in infrastructure and a plethora of new hotels, trendy bars and upmarket restaurants has created a resort that's more family-friendly than hedonistic yet still retains its title as nightlife centre of the island. Moving north, zones morph from the trendy Safari Centre shopping mall and Playa El Camisón to the still-jaded *CC Veronica's* at the imperceptible border with Costa Adeje.

Playa El Camisón

MAP P.74

A crescent of gently shelving sandy shoreline backed by a grassy embankment and protected from high waves by breakers, **Playa El Camisón** in the heart of Las Américas gets busy in high season but is still one of the nicest beaches in the south.

Costa Adeje

MAP P.77

Promoting itself as the upmarket alternative to its southern neighbours, the rapid development of **Costa Adeje** has centred around deluxe hotels springing up at a dizzying rate, fronted by manicured sands and bougainvillea-lined boulevards. In their wake,

at its del Duque end, overpriced restaurants and high-end shopping centres cater to the select few whose holiday budgets run to such exorbitant price tags. But it's not all swank and chic; venture south to parts of Torviscas and San Eugenio and remnants of the old Playa de Las Américas developments are still in evidence, with tacky souvenir shops, sports bars and touts.

Playa del Duque

MAP P.77

Cleaned, pressed and manicured to a five-star standard, sheltered **Playa del Duque** is the centrepiece of Costa Adeje's most exclusive

Playa del Duque

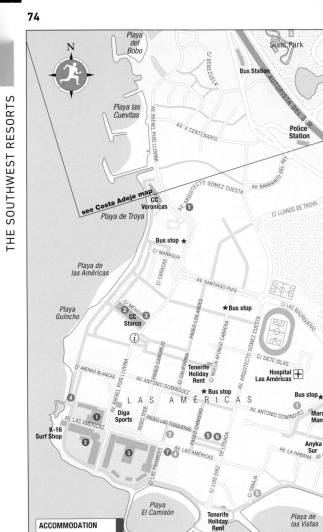

ACCOMMODATION

Andrea's	4
Europe Villa Cortes	1
Hard Rock Hotel	6
Parque Santiago III	2
Parque Santiago IV	3
Sensimar Arona Gran	5

RESTAURANTS

Arepa Gomerón	3
Casa Tagoro	6
El Cine	7
Hard Rock Cafe	4
Imperial Tai-Pan	2
Meson Castellano	1
Oliver's Out of Town	9
Otelo	8
Scampi's	5

BARS

Bull's Head	5
Dubliner Bar	3
OA Beach Club	4
Sax Bar	2

CLUB

Tramps	1

SHOWS

Carmen Mota Show, Pirámide de Arona	7
Brahms and Liszt Showbar	6

Las Américas and Los Cristianos

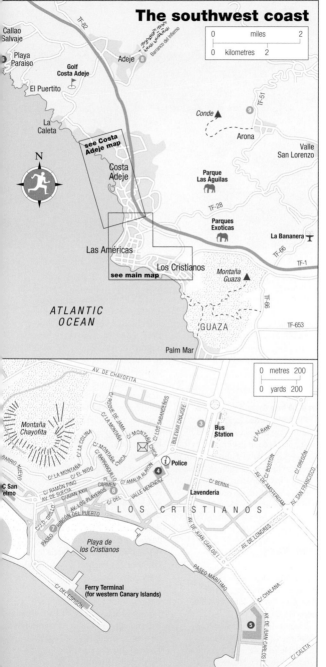

The southwest coast

| 0 | miles | 2 |
| 0 | kilometres | 2 |

Callao Salvaje
Playa Paraiso
El Puertito
Golf Costa Adeje
Adeje ⑧
Barranco del Infierno
TF-82
La Caleta
see Costa Adeje map
Costa Adeje
N
Conde ▲
Arona
TF-51
⑨
Valle San Lorenzo
Parque Las Águilas
TF-28
Las Américas
Los Cristianos
see main map
Parques Exoticas
La Bananera
TF-66
TF-1
Montaña Guaza ▲
TF-66
ATLANTIC OCEAN
GUAZA
TF-653
Palm Mar

| 0 | metres | 200 |
| 0 | yards | 200 |

AV. DE CHAYOFITA

Montaña Chayofita

BARRIO NUEVO

C/ ROQUE DE JAMA
C/ LA MONTAÑA
C/ MONTAÑA CHICA
C/ LOS SABANDEÑOS
BULEVAR CHAYOFE
③
Bus Station
C/ N-BAM-
C/ N-BAM-
C/ OREGON
AV. DE BOSTON
AV. DE AMSTERDAM
AV. SAN FRANCISCO

C/ LA MONTAÑA
C/ MONTAÑA CHICA
C/ CARNAVALITO
C/ AMALIA ALJON
ℹ️ Police ④
C/ BERNA
Lavenderia

C San Elmo
C/ RAMÓN PINO
AV. DE SUECIA
C/ JUAN XXIII
PL. CARMEN ⑥
C/ EL NIDO
VALLE MENENDEZ
C/ DEL
LOS CRISTIANOS

C/ D. DIEGO
PASEO ⑦
RINCÓN DEL PUERTO
AV. LOS PLAYEROS
AV. DE JUAN CARLOS I
AV. DE LONDRES

Playa de los Cristianos
PASEO MARÍTIMO
C/ CHALANA

C/ DEL ESPIGÓN
Ferry Terminal
(for western Canary Islands)
⑤
AV. DE JUAN CARLOS
C/ CALETA

Siam Park

neighbourhood. Thatched umbrellas and striped changing huts give the beach an almost Caribbean air, augmented by ocean views uncontaminated by the sprawl of Las Américas, which is obscured by the headland.

Palm-Mar

MAP P.74

Bus #468 from Guaza, 8 daily, 15min.
Beyond Montaña Guaza, on the southern tip of the island, there must have been ambitious plans for the development of **Palm-Mar**; they appear to have been shelved, though, leaving a half-constructed residential complex with little to offer the visitor. One of the only things worth heading here for is the lovely *Bahía Beach Bar* for *mojitos* at sunset.

Siam Park

MAP P.77

Av Siam Park, Adeje ☎ 822 07 00 00, ⓦ siampark.net. Daily: May–Oct 10am–6pm; Nov–Apr 10am–5pm. €38, under-11s €26.
A colossal dragon's head rising above the skyline alongside a Thai-style temple atop a stepped pyramid augurs what awaits at

Siam Park – consistently voted the world's number one water park by TripAdvisor. The many adrenaline rides include the Tower of Power slide, which plummets the brave an almost vertical 28m at speeds of up to 80mph. Those of a more nervous disposition can float lazily down the artificial Mekong river in a dinghy or stretch out on the Thai beach, complete with wave machine. In high season queues are prohibitive unless you invest in a fast track bracelet (€15). There are buses that pick up from locations across the island (€13.50 adults, €8 children); see the website for details.

La Caleta and El Puertito

MAP P.74

On foot along Geranium Walk, 1hr 30min–2hr if starting from Los Cristianos. Bus #467 from Costa del Silencio (via Los Cristianos, Las Américas & Costa Adeje) every 20min, 1hr.
Swamped by the voracious expansion of Costa Adeje, the former fishing village of **La Caleta** still manages to retain its traditional character – just. A small harbour tucked into the coastline beyond Playa de la Enramada, fish and

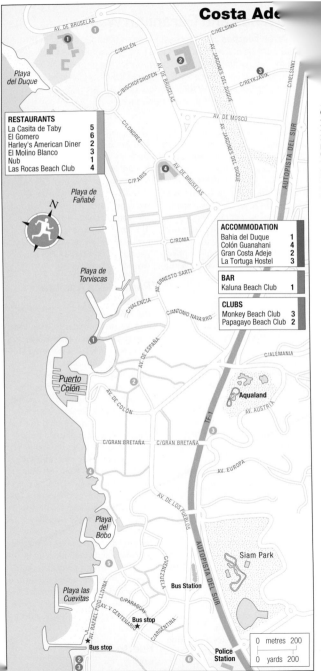

Costa Ade

RESTAURANTS

La Casita de Taby	5
El Gomero	6
Harley's American Diner	2
El Molino Blanco	3
Nub	1
Las Rocas Beach Club	4

ACCOMMODATION

Bahia del Duque	1
Colón Guanahani	4
Gran Costa Adeje	2
La Tortuga Hostel	3

BAR

Kaluna Beach Club	1

CLUBS

Monkey Beach Club	3
Papagayo Beach Club	2

Playa del Duque

Playa de Fañabé

Playa de Torviscas

Puerto Colón

Playa del Bobo

Playa las Cuevitas

Aqualand

Siam Park

Bus Station

Bus stop

Bus stop

Police Station

AV. DE BRUSELAS
C/HELSINKI
C/BAILÉN
C/BISCHOFSHOFEN
AV. DE BRUSELAS
AV. JARDINES DEL DUQUE
C/REYKJAVIK
C/HELSINKI
C/LONDRES
AV. DE MOSCÚ
AV. JARDINES DEL DUQUE
AUTOPISTA DEL SUR
C/P.ARIS
AV. DE BRUSELAS
C/ROMA
AV. ERNESTO SARTI
C/VALENCIA
C/ANTONIO NAVARRO
AV. DE ESPAÑA
C/ALEMANIA
AV. DE COLÓN
AV. AUSTRIA
TF-1
C/GRAN BRETAÑA
C/GRAN BRETAÑA
AV. EUROPA
AV. DE LOS PUEBLOS
AUTOPISTA DEL SUR
C/VENEZUELA
AV. RAFAEL PUIG LLUVINA
C/PARAGUAY
AV. V CENTENARIO
C/ARGENTINA
N

0	metres	200
0	yards	200

aches and Geranium Walk

A dozen **beaches** line the coast between Montaña Guaza at the southern tip of Los Cristianos and La Caleta in the west. Ranging from pristine and sandy to wild and rocky, the promenade which joins them all stretches for a whopping 9.5km and is known locally as **Geranium Walk** – though there are actually few geraniums to be seen along it nowadays.

seafood restaurants line the quay, their tables constantly buzzing with diners. Alongside, more upmarket restaurants are cashing in on La Caleta's popularity. Further up the headland the small, sheltered bay of **El Puertito** remains undeveloped, although plans to build another hotel have been mooted. For now, the cove with its black-sand beach backed by a clutch of whitewashed houses is a favourite summer venue for Canarian caravanners.

Callao Salvaje

MAP P.74
us #477 from Los Cristianos (via Las Américas and Costa Adeje) every 30min, 35min.

A small, unassuming coastal resort at the northern extreme of Costa Adeje, **Callao Salvaje** has a handful of restaurants and bars, a nice little black-sand and pebble beach and a smattering of hotels, villas and holiday apartments. More attractive than its neighbour, Playa Paraiso, its low-key profile mainly attracts mature couples and young families. Unless you're happy to do very little, you'll need a car.

Playa Paraiso

MAP P.74
Bus #477 from Los Cristianos (via Las Américas and Costa Adeje) to Las Cancelas and then a 30min walk; every 30min, 35min.

The opening of the *Hard Rock Hotel* gave **Playa Paraiso** a much-needed boost in its economic fortunes. But outside the resorts, it can still feel like a parody of its name – which translates as Paradise Beach – consisting predominantly of abandoned construction sites,

vacant shop fronts and one or two Brit bars that may have been the bee's knees back in the 1980s but are now deeply unattractive. Visitors to the area mainly confine themselves to their five-star, all-inclusive hotels with little beyond the front doors to entice them out. The small Playa de las Galgas at the foot of the cliffs provides sheltered swimming, as do the Lago Paraiso swimming pools.

Parque Las Águilas–Jungle Park

MAP P.74
Urbanización Las Águilas del Teide, Arona ⓦ junglepark.es. Daily 10am–5.30pm. €28, 5–10 year-olds €20, 3–4 year-olds €11 (tickets €2 cheaper online).

Parque Las Águilas–Jungle Park is one of southern Tenerife's premier attractions, with a sizeable collection of animal enclosures chaotically organized amid the lush vegetation of its replicated jungle. Despite its size and popularity, though, note that a few **animal welfare** concerns have still been raised, particularly regarding the ongoing sea lion performances. The main attractions are the bird shows, especially the displays of birds of prey who swoop low over the crowds; be aware that on windy days these shows are likely to be cancelled. Bring a picnic if you want to avoid the rather overpriced restaurants and cafés. There are free shuttle buses from locations across the island, check the website for details.

Puerto Colón

MAP P.77

In San Eugenio, Costa Adeje; 1hr 15min from Los Cristianos along Geranium Walk. Boat hire, fishing trips and whale- and dolphin-watching excursions are all available from **Puerto Colón** where a glut of advertising boards backed by ticket offices line the quay of the shiny marina. Alongside, rails of clothes and restaurant tables spill onto the quayside from the ground level of a small shopping centre. Beyond Club Náutico yacht club, the sun loungers of **Playa Colón** teem with sunbathers.

Adeje

MAP P.74
us #447 or #473 from Las Américas and Los Cristianos, 36 daily, 45min; bus #473 from Los Gigantes, 15 daily, 55min.
Above the coast and regularly shrouded in low cloud, the small administrative capital of **Adeje** is barely touched by tourism. Most visitors only come here for one of two reasons – to hike the Barranco del Infierno or to eat the garlic chicken. En route, it's worth checking out either the fortified hacienda of Casa Fuerte – a former slave market sacked by Sir Francis

Drake in 1586 and destroyed by fire in 1902 – and the simply decorated sixteenth-century Iglesia de Santa Ursula.

Barranco del Infierno hike

MAP P.74
C/Molinos 46, Adeje ⓦ barrancodelinfierno. es. Entrance daily 8–11.30am, closes 2.30pm; you are advised to arrive 15mins ahead of your reservation. Adults €11, Children €5.50.
The most popular **hike** on Tenerife due to its proximity to southern resorts, environmental and safety concerns limit daily visitors to **Barranco del Infierno** (Hell's Ravine) to just 20 people every half hour, so reservations are essential. The 6km/3.5 -hour return hike begins uphill of the Casa Fuerte in Adeje just beyond restaurant *Otelo* and follows the ravine through a varied landscape where semi-desert gives way to thick stands of willow and eucalyptus trees before finishing at a rather disappointing waterfall. Following heavy rain the *barranco* closes, so it's best to check before travelling, and see the website for restrictions on footwear.

Barranco del Infierno hike

Restaurants

Arepa Gomerón

MAP P.74

Avda Juan Carlos I 3, Los Cristianos ☎ 922 75 13 77, Mon–Fri 7am–9pm, Sat 7am–4.30pm.

Most non-Spanish speakers opt for something from the traditional Canarian menu whilst locals are more likely to order the *arepas* – small Venezuelan corn-flour pancakes stuffed with various fillings. Try the *carne machada* – spicy shredded beef. £

La Casita de Taby

MAP P.77

Centro Comercial Salytien, Avda Rafael Puig Lluvina, Costa Adeje ☎ 651 98 87 57. Wed 6pm–midnight, Thu–Mon 1pm–midnight.

In the absence of authentic tapas bars in the resort, *La Casita de Taby's* makes for a friendly, cosy alternative – plus there are sea views. The menu includes many tapas favourites such as *tortilla*, *papas bravas* and *boquerones* at low prices. £

Hard Rock Cafe

El Cine

MAP P.74

C/Juan Bariajo 8, Los Cristianos, ⓦ grupoelcine.com. Tue–Sun noon–11pm.

A Los Cristianos institution hidden away in a tiny alley opposite the port. The food is fresh and simply prepared; fish, seafood, and a chicken dish thrown in to appease people who don't like either. Great value mains but expect to queue. £

El Gomero

MAP P.77

Avda. Centenario 1, Costa Adeje ☎ 922 78 73 10. Mon–Sat 8am–11pm.

Authentic Canarian restaurants are somewhat of a rarity in Tenerife's purpose-built resorts, which is why this one is popular with taxi drivers and the local police. Good value, with large portions. £

Hard Rock Cafe

MAP P.74

Avda Las Américas, Playa de Las Américas ⓦ hardrock.com/cafes/Tenerife. Daily 5pm–11pm for the restaurant.

The *Hard Rock Cafe* personality fits in perfectly with the Vegas style of the area around the Safari shopping centre. This is the place to enjoy beefy burgers with a rocking soundtrack against a backdrop of mock Roman columns topped by a row of female archers. ££

Harley's American Diner

MAP P.77

Avda de España 3, Costa Adeje ⓦ harleystenerife.com. Wed–Sun 4pm–midnight.

Burgers, wraps and breakfasts in a kitsch (but fun) American-themed diner, with live music in the evenings from 10pm. There's a Fat Boy Burger challenge every Wed night for those with outsized appetites. £

Imperial Tai-Pan

MAP P.74

Centro Comercial Safari, Avda Las Américas 5, Playa de Las Américas ⓦ imperialtaipanrestaurant.com. Daily 1.30–11pm.

One of the Venture Group's restaurants, which means reliably good quality with prices on the more expensive side. In this case the focus is on Asian cuisine, with the menu including gourmet Chinese and Japanese dishes. The three-course imperial banquet for two is best value. £

Meson Castellano

MAP P.74

Avda Antonio Dominguez 38–40, Playa de Las Américas ☏ 922 79 21 36. Mon–Sat 1pm–midnight.

Generally considered one of the best Spanish restaurants on Tenerife, *Meson Castellano* isn't a good choice for vegetarians. This is a meat-eater's emporium, with a menu including Castilian classics such as Segovian suckling pig. £–££

El Molino Blanco

MAP P.77

Avda Austria 5, Costa Adeje ☏ 922 79 62 82, Ⓦ molino-blanco.com. Daily 2pm–midnight.

The menu features a range of international crowd-pleasers such as prawn cocktail and stroganoff, as well as a few Canarian dishes. The surroundings include leafy courtyards and a windmill, and there's a singing chef. A pricey venue combining dinner with live entertainment, including a pianist and singer. £

Nub

MAP P.77

Gran Hotel Bahía del Duque Resort, Avda de Bruselas, Costa Adeje Ⓦ nubrestaurante. com. Tue–Sat 6.30–9.30pm

Having moved from La Laguna, the restaurant's Michelin star was revalidated at this new venue in 2022. The Italian/Chilean husband and wife chef team combine techniques from their countries to elevate the already delicious local produce to a whole new level. Booking essential. ££££

Oliver's Out of Town

MAP P.74

Carretera General 51, Arona, Ⓦ olivers. paperless.menu. Tues–Sat 6.30–11pm.

For a long time this was the most popular restaurant in Los Cristianos, then in 2019 they moved to the picturesque village of Arona. It has become one of the 'must-do' gastronomic destinations on Tenerife. advance booking is highly recommended, and as far in advance as possible. The menu has a distinctly British gastropub grub feel to it, including the likes of Thai-style fish cakes and chicken breast stuffed with haggis. ££

Otelo

MAP P.77

C/los Molinos 44, Adeje Ⓦ otelorestaurante. com Wed–Mon 1–10pm.

Ordering food at *Otelo* is simplicity itself – grab a table with views overlooking the Barranco del Infierno, order the local speciality *pollo al ajillo* (garlic chicken) and relax. There are other Canarian dishes on the menu, but most people are there for the chicken. £

Las Rocas Beach Club

MAP P.77

C/Gran Bretaña, Costa Adeje Ⓦ dreamsjardintropical.com/restaurantes. Daily 1–3.30pm & 6.30–11pm.

Las Rocas Beach Club is part of the *Hotel Jardín Tropical*, but it doesn't feel like it as it sits apart from the hotel in a romantic spot jutting out over the sea; one of the best places in the resort for a sunset meal. Dishes are nicely prepared and presented, with main courses focused on seafood. ££

Scampi's

MAP P.74

Paseo Tarajal, Playa de Las Américas ☏ 922 75 32 32. Mon–Fri 1–9pm.

It might be unashamedly British on a Spanish island, but for anyone seeking familiar comfort food the undeniably good fish and chips at *Scampi's* will hit the spot. Cod and chips as good as any you will find in the UK. £

Bars

Bull's Head

MAP P.74

C/Luis Diaz de Losada 2, Playa de Las Américas ☎ 659 64 23 81. Daily 7pm–2am.

Bull's Head is one bar on a strip of bars known as 'The Patch', with live music of varying quality covering several genres. The main band here, Vagabonds, stand out from the crowd with their high-energy delivery of rock classics.

Dubliner Bar

MAP P.74

C/México, Playa de Las Américas ⓦ thedublineririshbar.com. Daily 11am–3am.

A dependable source of good craic, this is the best of the Irish bars hereabouts, with a lively and fun atmosphere and excellent resident band that has the whole crowd on their feet.

Kaluna Beach Club

MAP P.77

CC Centro Costa Local 79, Costa Adeje ⓦ kalunabeachclub.com. Wed–Sun 11am–8pm.

Kaluna Beach Club

Stylish chillout bar with DJs, VIP cabins and a pool overlooking the sea. The crowd at *Kaluna Beach Club* includes people who partied through the nineties at clubs in *CC Veronica's* and are now seeking a more relaxed scene, hence the early closing time.

OA Beach Club

MAP P.74

Paseo Francisco Andrade Fumero 1, Playa de la Américas, ⓦ europe-hotels. org/hoteles/villa-cortes/oa. Daily 11am–10.30pm

OA stands for 'Océano Atlántico' and this place is all about the stellar beachfront location. Needless to say, it's a great place to watch the often stunning sunset with a cocktail before enjoying a meal in the restaurant.

Sax Bar

MAP P.74

C/México 3, Playa de Las Américas ☎ 680 83 14 88. Tue–Sun 9pm–2am.

Despite the bar's name, *Sax Bar*'s house band play mainly classic rock covers from the Rolling Stones to the Kings of Leon. A good holiday live music bar.

Clubs

Monkey Beach Club

MAP P.77
Avda Rafael Puig Lluvina 3, Costa Adeje
Ⓦ monkeybeachclub.com. Daily 1–11pm.
The place which started the beach club trend in the south of Tenerife. Sitting above the sands of Playa Troya, it still boasts the best beachside location. Like others it also serves food and is a popular cocktail-sipping sunset venue. The liveliest time to visit is during the summer season, when the Sunday-night beach parties (held mid-June to early Oct) attract locals and visitors alike.

Papagayo Beach Club

MAP P.74
Avda Rafael Puig Lluvina 2, Playa de Las
Américas Ⓦ papagayobeachclub.com.
Wed–Sun 4pm–midnight.
Papagayo Beach Club manages to seamlessly blend three different sides to its personality over the course of 24 hours – classy beachside lunch spot during the day, sunset cocktail bar in the early evening and club featuring the best of local and international DJs at night.

Tramps

MAP P.74
CC Starco, Avda Arquitecto Gómez Cuesta,
Playa de Las Américas Ⓦ trampstenerife.
com. Daily 10pm–6am.
With three large rooms playing house, R&B, and retro sounds from the eighties, nineties and noughties, *Tramps* retains its crown as Tenerife's king of clubs.

Shows

Brahms And Liszt Cabaret Showbar

MAP P.74
C/Luis Diaz de Losada, Playa de Las
Américas Ⓦ brahmsandliszt.weebly.com
Mon–Sat 11am–1am, Sun 11am–midnight.

Bar in Playa de las Americas

Perhaps not the most inspired venue name, but the team have been entertaining crowds in Tenerife for well over 20 years, so they must be doing something right. In the early evening this is a fun place to catch any live sports events, after which it then transforms into the area's most flamboyant cabaret night.

Carmen Mota Show, Pirámide de Arona

MAP P.74
Mare Nostrum Resort, Playa de Las
Américas Ⓦ marenostrumresort.com.
Performances Tues, Thurs, Fri & Sat 9pm
& Wed 8pm.
Carmen Mota's slickly choreographed shows at *Pirámide de Arona* feature a flamboyant fusion of traditional and contemporary flamenco and are a swirling head and shoulders above anything else in the main southwestern resort area. The theme of the show changes regularly, but the ingredients always remain the same. Prices start at €49. For quality, foot-stomping flamenco, this show is one not to be missed.

The southeast coast

Tenerife's mass tourism began in the 1960s with the construction of *Ten-Bel*, a sprawling concrete holiday complex which hugs the rocky shoreline east of the beach and marina of Las Galletas. Amazingly it's still in business, albeit under a new name, despite barely a lick of paint in the intervening years. Bereft of a decent beach and with a default setting of sunny and windy, the coast spreads eastwards along Costa del Silencio in a sea of bland, uniform holiday apartments until it meets the greens of Golf del Sur, beyond which it redeems itself in El Médano. Wind- and kite-surfing capital of the island, El Médano's sandy beaches are the last thing visitors see as their planes take off over Montaña Roja.

Las Galletas

MAP P.86

The highlight of Tenerife's south-easterly tip, **Las Galletas** has refused to let the mass tourism that begins on its doorstep taint its fishing village roots. The lack of any sizeable accommodation leaves the sheltered sand-and-pebble beach devoid of crowds and allows the town to focus on what it does best – fishing,

sailing and diving. Every morning the daily catch is sold from stalls behind the marina, from where it makes its way to the kitchens of the fish and seafood restaurants along the pier and promenade. Nestled behind the coastal front line, fishermen's cottages sit cheek by jowl with restaurants and dive schools before morphing into a small shopping centre.

Las Galletas

Arrival and Information

There are several useful **bus routes** running from Tenerife South airport: bus #415 (hourly, 50mins) goes to Las Galletas via Golf del Sur; #111 (frequent, 25min) runs to Los Cristianos, from where #467 (frequent, 35min) heads to Costa del Silencio and #470 (hourly) to Los Abrigos (50min) and El Médano (1hr). El Médano is best accessed by **taxi** (approx €25), though, as bus routes there are convoluted.

Las Galletas' **tourist information** booth (Mon–Fri 9am–3pm; ☎ 922 73 01 33) is on pedestrianized La Rambla, behind the seafront promenade. In El Médano, the helpful tourist information booth (Mon–Sat 9am–4.30pm; ☎ 922 17 60 02) is on the north side of Plaza Principe de Asturias. In Golf del Sur, there's a tourist information office on Avenida José Miguel Galván Bello, on the main road into the resort (Mon–Fri 8am–3pm; ☎ 922 73 86 64).

Rusted wrecks, deep caverns and volcanic undersea formations teeming with life make for excellent **diving** in the seas off Las Galletas (see page 133 for information on diving centres).

Costa del Silencio

MAP P.86

Bus #110 from Santa Cruz to Los Cristianos (every 30min, 55min), then change to #467 (very frequent, 35min).

An expansive mass of homogenous hotels interspersed with holiday housing developments stretches along the rocky **Costa del Silencio** from beyond *Ten-Bel* to Montaña Amarilla, with little to redeem it. Three small commercial centres include supermarkets, bars and restaurants appealing predominantly to British tastes.

Montaña Amarilla

MAP P.86

A path leads from beyond Amarilla Bay apartments in Costa del Silencio to the base of **Montaña Amarilla**. Alternatively, it's a nice coastal walk (9km/2hr 40min return), beginning at Marina San Miguel in Amarilla Golf. Formed from continual erosion on the volcanic cone revealing fossilized sand dunes, the mountain is a cross

section of layered bands of gold with small exposed shelves of rock on which sunbathers acquire an all-over tan. Opposite, the same eroded rock shelves provide a panoramic chillout zone, complete with a mellow beach bar.

Golf del Sur

MAP P.86

Like much of this part of the coast, the hotels, homes and apartments of **Golf del Sur** predominantly attract the British, who come to enjoy its sunny climate and its golf courses, bright flashes of green amid the barren natural environment. Catering to their needs, Indian restaurants, wine bars and sports-coverage TV screens dominate the resort's commercial centre. Within Golf del Sur is the tiny resort of *Amarilla Golf*, which comprises little more than the greens of its golf course and is where the San Miguel Marina is located.

Los Abrigos

MAP P.86

Bus #470 from Los Cristianos via Golf del Sur & Las Galletas, hourly, 50min.

Defiantly traditional amid the sea of new developments to its west, the little harbour of **Los Abrigos**

Kite boarding, El Médano

has been specialising in fish and seafood for half a century and continues to do so, attracting

locals and visitors to its bustling harbourside. Every Tuesday a handful of stalls sets up for the night market (5–9pm), selling jewellery, leather goods and clothes.

El Médano

MAP P.86
Bus #470 from Los Cristianos (hourly, 1hr); #111 from Santa Cruz to Los Cardones (every 30min, 55min), then #411 (5 daily, 10min).

The most laidback of south Tenerife's resorts, **El Médano**'s near constant breeze attracts wind- and kite-surfers from across Europe – it hosts the annual PWA World Cup. Managing to retain its *tinerfeño* culture alongside its surf dude ambience, El Médano boasts the best beaches on Tenerife – natural golden sands, some of which are dominated by the sails of windsurfers, while others have the capacity to turn sunbathers into

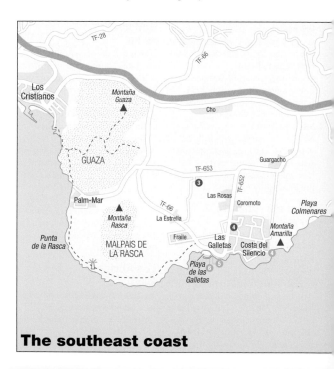

The southeast coast

Submarine Safaris

Departing from the San Miguel Marina, **Submarine Safaris** (☎ 922 73 66 29, ⓦ submarinesafaris.com; Mon–Fri & Sun 9am–7pm; €57 including pick-up from south Tenerife, €69 from north Tenerife; children €35/€42; ten percent online discount) runs trips in a bright, modern **submarine** with large viewing portals and maintained cabin pressure, diving to a depth of 30m (100ft). The onboard **guides** provide a commentary on sightings which might include barracuda, parrot fish and rays. Free buses pick up from Playa de Las Américas, Los Cristianos and Los Gigantes; see their website for details.

sand sculptures on windy days. Life mainly revolves around the town beach and Plaza Principe de Asturias and its surrounding streets, where restaurants and cafés serve eclectic menus often including vegetarian options, and neo-hippies sell hand-made jewellery from stalls. Alongside its sandy coastline, a boardwalk runs the length of the resort backed by bars and cafés, plus shops selling surf-related clothing and paraphernalia.

Montaña Roja

MAP P.86

A walk along El Médano's boardwalk and the shoreline beyond takes you to the resort's emblematic **Montaña Roja**, a 171m-tall, red volcanic cone in

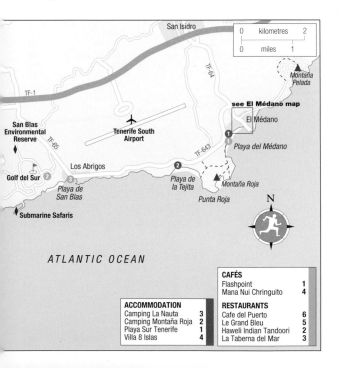

San Blas environmental reserve

Sandwiched between the golf courses of Golf del Sur and the harbour of Los Abrigos, the small **environmental reserve of San Blas** is an oasis of preserved *malpaís* in a desert of development. Protected from any kind of construction or agricultural interference, the space is filled with volcanic cones amid lava fields and contains a small, bright green lake whose colour comes from the algae that grows in it. Occupying the edge of the reserve, the *Sandos San Blas* hotel offers **guided tours** (ⓦnew.sandos.com/ sandos-san-blas/environmental-reserve; tours Mon–Thurs & Sun 9.45am, 10.15am & 11.45am, book at reception); they start with a film explaining the volcanic formation of the island, then involve a walk through the reserve including crossing the lake on a raft operated by a rope pulley. Audio guides (several languages) provide commentary about the landscape, flora and fauna, and local actors provide Guanche cameo scenes during the walk. The tour is rounded off with a surround-screen video experience.

the centre of a nature reserve protecting a dune ecosystem. One easily followed path from the western end of El Médano's beach leads through this area to the summit (2.5km/40min), while another rounds the hill on its inland side and leads to a beautiful but windswept beach, **Playa de la Tejita**.

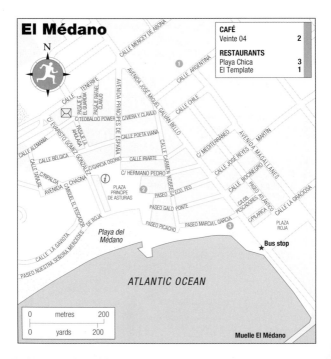

Cafés

Flashpoint
MAP P.86

C/Nuestra Señora Mercedes de Roja 52,
El Médano ☎ 922 17 61 11. Sun–Thu
9.30am–10pm, Fri & Sat 9.30am–11pm.
By the beach at the western end of
town, this trendy café with a terrace
serves excellent breakfasts, and rolls
and pizzas in the afternoon. The
evening menu is meat or fish fillets
served with salad and rice. Great
place to watch wind- and kite-surfers.

Mana Nui Chiringuito
MAP P.86

Montaña Amarilla, Costa del Silencio. Mon
& Wed–Sun noon–8pm.
Little more than a shed on the rocks
by the distinctive Montaña Amarilla,
Mana Nui Chiringuito serves teas,
cocktails, ice creams and snacks. With
its rock seating and naturally surreal
surroundings, this unusual *chiringuito*
(beach bar) is in complete contrast to
the resort which hides it from view.

Veinte 04
MAP P.86

Plaza Principe de Asturias, El Médano
Ⓦ veinte04.com. Sun & Tue–Thu 9.30am–
11pm, Fri & Sat 9.30am–midnight.
Occupying pole position on the
plaza, *Veinte 04* "surf café" is an El
Médano establishment which affords
great people-watching. The varied
menu includes dishes ranging from
ceviche and *calamari* to burgers.

Restaurants

Café del Puerto
MAP P.86

Puerto Deportivo Marina del Sur Cl
Rambla de Dionisio González, Las Galletas
Ⓦ cafedelpuerto-restaurant.negocio.site.
Mon noon–6pm, Wed–Sun noon–8pm
Family-run restaurant offering great
value fish and seafood, especially
considering the prime location
right on the marina. Meat dishes
also available. £

Le Grand Bleu
MAP P.86

Paseo Marítimo, Rambla Dionisio González,
Las Galletas ☎ 655 70 85 47. Tue–Sat
9.30am–3pm & 7–10pm, Sun 9.30am–3pm.
There are clear Belgian/French
influences in some restaurants in
Las Galletas. Try *Le Grand Bleu*,
with a fine-dining menu which
includes *moules Provençale* and
magret de canard in port sauce. £

Haweli Indian Tandoori
MAP P.86

CC San Blas, Golf del Sur ☎ 922 73 82 09.
Daily noon–3pm & 6pm–midnight.
British favourites are what Golf
del Sur does best. Friendly,
unpretentious *Haweli Indian
Tandoori* is better than most of the
Indian restaurants dotted around
the southern resorts; the three-
course set menu is great value. £

Playa Chica
MAP P.86

Paseo Marcial Garcia 32, El Médano ☎ 922
17 92 62. Daily 8am–11pm.
Colourful tapas and fish restaurant
beside the small beach of the same
name. *Playa Chica* is a charming
spot to lunch on a selection of
raciones beside the sea. £

La Taberna del Mar
MAP P.86

Calle La Marina 22, Los Abrigos ☎ 822 10
57 97. Mon–Wed, Fri & Sat 12.30–9pm, Sun
12.30–5pm.
The Galician-style Canarian dishes
in this harbourside restaurant make
it popular with locals and visitors.
Prices are good for the quality. The
platter of mixed fried seafood is
popular as a sharing dish. £

El Templete
MAP P.86

CC El Médano nivel 1, El Médano ☎ 922 17 60
79. Tues–Sat 1–4pm & 7.30–11pm, Sun 1–4pm.
In a nondescript shopping centre,
El Templete is for those seeking good
food rather than great views; its
reputation for quality cuisine draws
locals from across the island. £

Teide and the interior

Standing at 3718m, beneath one of the world's clearest skies and within the 16km-wide crater of Parque Nacional Las Cañadas del Teide, Mount Teide is the largest mountain in Spain and the third tallest volcano on the planet. The lava fallout from successive eruptions combined with atmospheric conditions within the park create a surreal, kaleidoscopic canvas surrounded by a sea of clouds and the site is considered of such global importance that it has been a Unesco World Heritage Site since 2007. The literal and experiential highlight of any visit to the Canary Islands, many of its 4 million annual visitors travel from the coastal resorts of the south and ride the cable car to within 200m of the summit, completely unprepared for the freezing temperatures into which they then step out.

Vilaflor

MAP P.92
Bus #482 from Los Cristianos, 3 daily, 1hr 15min.

Alpine **Vilaflor** is a former spa town and birthplace of Tenerife's only saint, a goatherd named Pedro who moved to Guatemala and founded the Bethlehemites. The town sits in pine forest on the cusp of the national park and makes a fine base from which to explore Teide and its environs. Cloudless days afford widescreen views from the village across the whole south coast, but when the mist descends, temperatures quickly fall – visitors are advised to dress in layers. Flower-lined streets lead to the pretty plaza and Iglesia de San Pedro, whose namesake saint stands alongside a sculptural fountain and from where the route to Paisaje Lunar begins.

El Portillo Visitor Centre

MAP P.92
Parque National del Teide, where the TF21 from La Orotava meets the TF24 from La Laguna ☎ 922 92 23 71. Daily 9am–4.15pm. Free.

Arrival and information

It's easiest to get to the national park by **car**, though there are daily **buses** from Las Américas and Los Cristianos (#342, 1 daily each way, 1hr 40min; departs 9.15am from Las Américas bus station, calls at Los Cristianos and returns 3.15pm from El Portillo Visitor Centre, calling at the cable car and Parador) and from Puerto de la Cruz (#348, 1 daily each way, 1hr 45min; departs 9.30am from Puerto and returns 4pm from the Parador, calling at the cable car and El Portillo Visitor Centre).

Only one **road** (TF21) runs through the crater of Parque National del Teide, accessed by four subsidiary roads: the TF38 which ascends from the west via Chio; the TF21 which ascends from the south via Vilaflor; the TF21 from the north that ascends from La Orotava; and the TF24 from La Laguna which links up with the TF21 from La Orotava at the El Portillo Visitor Centre.

Inside the **El Portillo Visitor Centre** is where your volcano experience begins, as you cross a mock volcanic tube with molten lava running beneath your feet to reach interactive displays on vulcanology, geology, flora and fauna, plus maps and leaflets about the generally well-marked hiking trails. There are also spectacular photographic displays and videos of erupting volcanoes. The centre also organizes free **guided hikes** of varying difficulty. There's a second, smaller centre (same hours) beside the Parador on the south side of the park that concentrates on the park's human heritage. There is adequate, free parking on the road outside and there are public toilets.

Paisaje Lunar

MAP P.92
Bus #482 from Los Cristianos, 3 daily, 1hr 15min

Half a million years of fallout from successive volcanic eruptions, that rained down on the slopes of the *barranco* and solidified, has been sculpted and moulded by wind and rain erosion to create spectral columns of volcanic cinders and ash that pepper the side of the valley like petrified aliens. A well-marked **trail** (14.5km, 4hr 50min return) begins from Plaza de San Pedro in **Vilaflor** and climbs the old Camino de Chasna trading route into the pine forest to reach a viewing platform over the protected **Paisaje Lunar**. You can shorten the route by joining it from the road between Vilaflor and Parque National del Teide but you'll miss some of the nicest parts by doing so.

Altavista Refuge

MAP P.92
Mount Teide ⓦ volcanoteide.com. Nightly 5pm–8am. Booking is advisable & can be done online; only one night's stay is permitted. From €26.

Based at 3260m on the side of Mount Teide, **Altavista** is the highest refuge in Spain and staying here is a unique experience, one that allows you to witness a spectacular sunset and one of the clearest night skies on the planet. Accommodation is basic and there are no showering facilities. There are vending machines to buy water, soft drinks and hot drinks but you will need coins for them. There are some limited cooking facilities but

Canarian pine forest

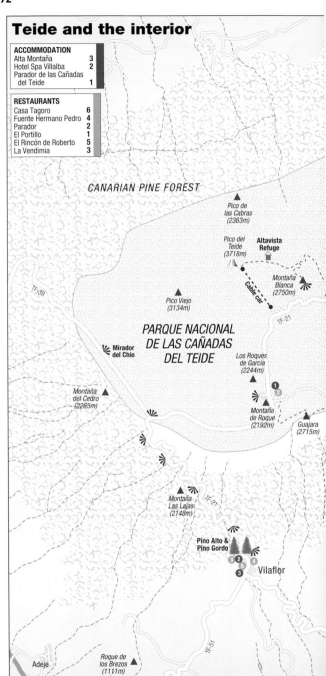

Teide and the interior

ACCOMMODATION

Alta Montaña	3
Hotel Spa Villalba	2
Parador de las Cañadas del Teide	1

RESTAURANTS

Casa Tagoro	6
Fuente Hermano Pedro	4
Parador	2
El Portillo	1
El Rincón de Roberto	5
La Vendimia	3

CANARIAN PINE FOREST

Pico de las Cabras (2363m)

Pico del Teide (3718m)

Altavista Refuge

Montaña Blanca (2750m)

Cable Car

Pico Viejo (3134m)

TF-38

TF-21

PARQUE NACIONAL DE LAS CAÑADAS DEL TEIDE

Mirador del Chio

Los Roques de García (2244m)

Montaña del Cedro (2265m)

Montaña de Roque (2192m)

Guajara (2715m)

Montaña Las Lajas (2148m)

TF-21

Pino Alto & Pino Gordo

Vilaflor

Adeje

Roque de los Brezos (1111m)

TF-51

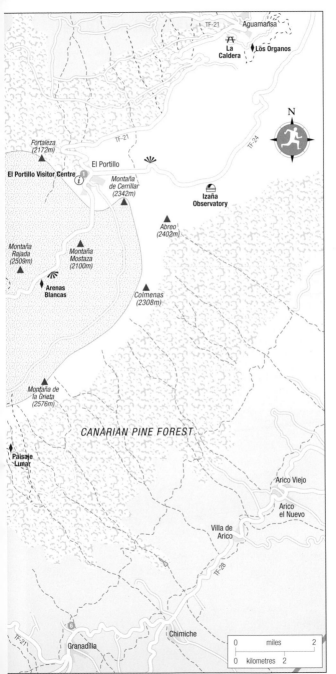

Hiking in Parque National del Teide

Tenerife's most popular day trip destination, crowds flock to Parque National del Teide but rarely wander far from their excursion coaches and the cable car. Taking to the park's multiple waymarked **trails** (pick up a free map at the visitor centres) is an easy way to find yourself a spot devoid of other people, where you can really experience this extraordinary landscape. There are few days when cloud covers the mountain; usually, even on the cloudiest days, once you get above 1500m you break through into clear, blue skies and in winter, although your boots are crunching on icy ground, you'll soon be down to a T-shirt. Always wear strong sunscreen and a hat when **hiking in Parque National del Teide** as there is virtually no shade; wear closed, robust trainers or hiking boots and carry one to one-and-a-half litres of water per person. It's advisable to always have good walking directions as well as a **map** – people frequently get lost while hiking in the park and risk hypothermia by having to spend the night at minus temperatures. Ensure you never leave valuables in the car, even for a very short time, as theft from vehicles is rife in this area.

Siete Cañadas – 16.5km, 4hr 30min

One of the easiest trails (number 4) in Parque National del Teide – the ground is relatively flat, with only a 500m or so ascent and descent, and the terrain is generally good – this path runs between the two visitor centres, crossing the eastern edge of the crater at the foot of the remaining crater wall. Joining up with several other marked trails, you can simply walk as far as you wish to and then turn back, or you can use the map to devise your own circular route.

La Forteleza – 10.6km, 3hr

Beginning from the back of the El Portillo Visitor Centre, this path (trails 1 & 24) takes you to the only remaining section of the north crater wall. Passing the blooms or skeletal spikes of *tajinaste rojo* en route, you either look out over the lush beauty of the north coast or over a sea of clouds depending on the weather below you.

Roques de García – 3.7km, 1hr 30min

Another easy trail (number 3), with a short, steep ascent and descent of 150m to begin and end. This route takes you below the iconic (it featured on the 1000 peseta note), shillelagh-shaped Roque Cinchado and into the Ucanca Plains. Passing the El Catedrál rock formation, a favourite with rock climbers, you get a very different perspective of the park on this path.

Alto de Guajara – 13.3km, 5hr

This testing yet spectacular route begins alongside the Parador by following Siete Cañadas (number 4) and then breaks off to climb the highest remaining section of the crater wall, Alto de Guajara (paths 5 & 15). Alongside the remains of the world's first high mountain observatory, views are over Mount Teide and the splendour of the Cañades.

Teide Summit – 7.2km, 7hr

Those with the stamina can choose to undertake the park's ultimate hike – to the peak of Mount Teide, which begins at the base of Montaña Blanca. You'll need a permit (see page 96) to access the peak itself – unless you choose to spend the night at the Altavista Refuge and climb in the dark, to witness sunrise from the summit and the shadow of Mount Teide cast across the sea of clouds (ensuring you're back beyond cable car level before 9am). This is a steep ascent on loose scree and at altitude and should not be undertaken lightly. The initial climb to the Altavista Refuge ascends 1000m over 7km and takes 4–5hr. The final 200m ascent to the summit can take 2hr or more due to the altitude.

Paisaje Lunar

if there are a lot of people staying they are in constant use. Bunks are in dormitories, each sleeping sixteen people, and sleeping bags are provided. Lights are turned out at 9pm and are turned on again at 5am as most people rise to begin the pre-dawn ascent to the peak. Dormitories close at 7.30am. Even though the dormitories are heated the refuge is cold, so ensure you bring adequate layers of clothing. If the mountain is icy the refuge and the trail to the summit may be closed; check before you begin your journey.

Teide by cable car

MAP P.92

☎ 922 01 04 40, ⓦ volcanoteide.com. Daily 9am–4pm. From €21.

Carrying 38 people at a time, the **Teleferico cable car** ascends 1200m in around seven minutes and deposits passengers just 200m below the peak of Mount Teide. From there, three routes begin: you can continue to the summit on foot, for which you'll need a permit (see page 96); you can head north to a viewpoint over **La Fortaleza** and the north coast; or you can head south to a viewpoint

The summit permit

Only **150 visitors a day** are allowed up to the eight-metre wide crater rim on the summit of Teide and the tiny sulphurous vents that surround it, and only 50 are allowed onto the trail at any one time. In order to progress beyond the upper cable car station (unless you stay overnight at the Altavista Refuge and ascend before daylight) you must be in possession of a valid **permit**. The path is chained and manned by a ranger who controls all access. You can apply online (ⓦ reservasparquesnacionales.es) for a free permit and can select a two-hour slot. Be aware if you choose the last slot of the day (3–5pm) that the last cable car back down is at 4.30pm. It's advisable to book as far in advance as you can, because slots fill up quickly.

Teide flora

Given the very unique conditions experienced in the Cañadas (under 500mm rain annually, regular ground frost and high levels of solar exposure), the **variety of flora** found in the crater and on the mountain has adapted to the conditions. Small leaves prevent loss of moisture through evaporation while compact forms protect against high winds. Of the 168 species of plants recorded in the park, 58 are endemic to the Canary Islands, with 33 unique to Tenerife and 12 to the park itself. Most prevalent is the Teide Retama (white broom) while unique endemics include a mauve wallflower (*Erysimum scoparium*). Three floral treasures of the park are the **Teide violet** (*Viola cheiranthifolia*), the **Teide edelweiss** (*Laphangium teydeum*) and the **Viper's bugloss** or *tajinaste rojo*, also known as Tower of Jewels (*Echium wildpretii*), which grows in crimson spikes to a height of 1.5m during May and June and has become a symbol of the park.

over **Pico Viejo**, an almost perfect volcanic crater worthy of being the lair of a Bond villain. Unless it's a rare, high-cloud day, whichever route you take you will be able to get satellite views over the neighbouring islands of La Gomera, La Palma and El Hierro in the west, and Gran Canaria in the east. At this height (3555m above sea level) you may experience symptoms of altitude sickness (headache, nausea) and should take time to sit and let your body adjust before exploring. Walk slowly and take plenty of rests. If symptoms persist, you should return to crater level as soon as possible. To minimize the invariable queues at the cable car it's best to try to get there as early as possible, before the coach excursions arrive. Alternatively, you could choose to go later in the afternoon, but the

Teide flora

Stargazing

Along with Chile and Hawaii, the Canary Islands are considered to have the **clearest skies** in the world and, given its height above sea level, Parque National del Teide is the best place on Tenerife to experience them. From here, on clear moonless nights, 83 of the 88 constellations have been observed. Those choosing to spend the night within the crater, either at the Parador or in the Altavista Refuge, will automatically enjoy dazzling night skies; however, you can also book a **Sunset & Stars tour** (From €80; or €125 including meal and cocktail; Ⓦvolcanoteide.com) to maximise your Teide-by-night experience. The cable car re-opens to take participants to the upper station, from where they witness sunset and the spectacle of Teide's shadow cast across the landscape. A gourmet meal and cocktails are then served in the lower cable car station, followed by a stargazing session led by experts.

last cable car back down leaves the upper station at 4.30pm. On windy days the cable car does not operate, so check online before setting out.

Izaña Observatory

MAP P.92
Parque National del Teide (follow signs from km37 of the TF24) Ⓦiac.es. Tours in English Mon, Tues & Thurs 2.30pm, Wed noon; 1hr 30min. €21.

First set up in the 1960s, **Izaña** is one of the largest solar observatories in the world and is where astrophysics in the Canaries began. Its geographical location between the eastern and western solar observatories, along with the clarity and air quality of the sky, make it ideal for observing the sun. **Tours** include observation of sunspots and solar flares and seeing the inside of a nocturnal telescope. You can arrange pick-up from Costa Adeje, Los Cristianos and Puerto de la Cruz at additional cost; see website.

Izaña Observatory

Restaurants

Casa Tagoro

MAP P.92

C/Tagoro 28, Granadilla ⓦ casatagoro.com.
Wed & Thu 7–11pm, Fri & Sat 1–4pm &
7–11pm, Sun 1–11pm.

Serving international cuisine
with an Austrian influence, the
owners of Casa Tagoro started
life in this restored 18th Century
townhouse and built a reputation
that had people visiting from all
over the island. Following a brief
relocation to Los Cristianos, they
have returned to their roots and
reopened the townhouse. This
feels like where they should be,
with the surroundings matching
the traditional Bavarian cuisine,
prepared with the same care and
attention that went into restoring
the building. £–££

Brunch with a view

Fuente Hermano Pedro

MAP P.92

Plaza Obispo Pérez Cáceres, Vilaflor ⓣ 922
70 93 60. Mon–Thu 9am–9pm, Sat & Sun
10am–9pm.

Located on Vilaflor's pretty main
plaza, with both indoor and outdoor
seating, this restaurant specializes
in traditional Canarian dishes but
is also good for *bocadillos* (filled
baguettes) or just a cool drink in
the sunshine. Prices are aimed at
canarios, so *conejo en salmorejo*
(rabbit in sauce) is great-value. £

Parador Hotel and Restaurant

MAP P.92

Parador las Cañadas del Teide, Parque
Nacional del Teide ⓦ parador.es/en/
paradores/parador-de-las-canadas-del-
teide. Daily 1.30–3pm & 7.30–10pm.

The dining room has panoramic
views of Mount Teide, as long
as you have a table near the
window, and the menu is an
interesting mix of traditional
and more contemporary dishes.
Portions, especially for the
starters, can be big. Given
its unique location prices are
actually very reasonable. ££

El Rincón de Roberto

MAP P.92

Avda Hermano Pedro 27, Vilaflor
ⓦ buenacarta.es/elrinconderoberto. Mon &
Tues 1–10pm, Fri–Sun 1–11pm.

Good traditional cuisine with a
mainland Spanish influence (the
owner is from Madrid). Try a
selection of local flavours in one
go by opting for the Canarian
platter. £

La Vendimia

MAP P.92

Hotel Spa Villalba Camino San Roque,
Vilaflor ⓦ hotelvillalba.com. Daily 8–10pm.

This restaurant is inside a rural
hotel on the edge of the pine forest,
and has a menu which includes
both international and tweaked
local dishes, many using ingredients
from the hotel's gardens. Dinner
is more of a sophisticated affair
than at other local restaurants,
and the wine from the family
bodega is worth trying. The menu
is extremely focused on wellbeing,
with the benefits of each ingredient
explained. £–££

San Sebastián and southern La Gomera

San Sebastián is La Gomera's capital and largest town. It was from here that Christopher Columbus set sail on September 6, 1492, on his momentous voyage to the Americas. In deference to that historic event, La Gomera has since referred to itself as Isla Columbiana (Columbus Island) although exploitation of its role is remarkably low key. Few of San Sebastián's historic buildings survived attacks by Dutch and British corsairs but its streets exude the tranquil air of a small, close–knit community and its beach is one of the island's best. On the sunny south coast, the resort of Playa de Santiago is dominated by the Olsen family's *La Tecina* hotel, holiday developments and a clifftop golf course. Below them, at the confluence of multiple *barrancos*, the restaurants, shops and cafés of the village line the small promenade alongside a leafy plaza.

Torre del Conde

MAP P.103
Parque de la Torre Del Conde ☎ 922 14 15 12. Mon–Fri 9am–1pm & 4–6pm, Sat & Sun 10am–5pm. Free.

San Sebastián's first building of any note was the stocky medieval **Torre del Conde** fort, built in 1447 to protect against attack from the island's Guanche, who were suffering under the despotic rule of the Spanish. The tower proved useful when Beatriz de Bobadilla, the wife of the murdered governor Hernán Peraza, barricaded herself in during a 1488 uprising until help arrived to save her.

Today the fort contains interesting displays on Gomeran history with maps from 1492 showing how, at the time when Columbus was striking out into unknown waters, most of the Gomeran interior was still uncharted – and would remain so until the seventeenth century.

Arrival and information

Regular **ferry services** by Fred Olsen and Naviera Armas are the easiest and cheapest way to get to La Gomera, connecting Tenerife's Los Cristianos to San Sebastián. There is also a small **airport** which connects the island to North Tenerife airport, convenient for access to Playa de Santiago. The town's **tourist office** (Mon–Fri 8am–3pm, ☎ 922 87 02 81) is in Casa Bencomo on Calle Real, near Casa Colón. There's also a much smaller office on Playa de Santiago's Avenida Maritima (Mon–Sat 9am–3pm ☎ 922 89 56 50). The official website ⓦ lagomera.travel also has a wealth of information.

Iglesia Nuestra Señora de la Asunción

MAP P.103
C/Real ☎ 922 87 03 03. Mass Mon, Wed, Fri & Sun 11am & 1pm.

Before setting off on his voyage, Columbus supposedly visited **Iglesia Nuestra Señora de la Asunción** for a final session of prayers. Construction of the building started in 1490 and took twenty years to complete, so it's difficult to imagine what it would have looked like in 1492. In any case, an attack by Algerian pirates in 1618 destroyed all but its basic structure, so today's church dates mostly from the seventeenth century – a brick-and-lime, mostly Gothic-style construction, with some Baroque elements, particularly in the carvings of the impressive wooden altars.

The archway to the left of the main entrance, called the **Puerta del Perdón**, is the doorway

Iglesia Nuestra Señora de la Asunción

through which the Guanches were invited to step for a full amnesty after their 1488 uprising. Hundreds

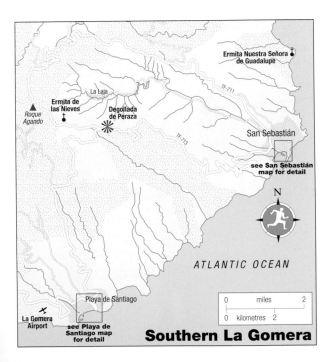

Beatriz de Bobadilla

Although La Gomera's most famous association is with Christopher Columbus, its most infamous is with the aristocratic **Beatriz de Bobadilla**. Beatriz was, by reputation, a vicious medieval nymphomaniac, and by all accounts – including her portrait in San Sebastián's Parador Nacional – a great beauty.

Once a mistress of King Ferdinand of Aragon, Beatriz was instantly disliked by his wife Queen Isabella of Castile, who feared her manipulative powers. Consequently, she was quickly married off to an equally out-of-favour Spanish aristocrat and banished to La Gomera – then the outermost island of the Spanish empire. The couple began a ferocious and brutal rule on the island, which led to uprisings and his death in 1488.

Four years later, in 1492, Beatriz played host to Christopher Columbus, who delayed his first journey to the New World for over a month, giving rise to much speculation about the pair. But eventually Beatriz married Alonso Fernández de Lugo, the conqueror of Tenerife. She lived there until rumours prompted her to order the execution of Gomera's governor; as a result, she was summoned to the Spanish court by Isabella. Within days of arrival Beatriz was found poisoned in bed; no real effort was made to investigate the death of the ruthless beauty.

came – only to find they had been tricked. They were subsequently either executed or sold as slaves.

Casa de Colón

MAP P.103

Torre del Conde

C/Real 56 ☎ 922 14 15 12. Mon–Wed & Fri 10am–4pm, Thu 10am–2pm. Free.
A traditional seventeenth-century house with wooden balconies and inner courtyard, the so-called **Casa de Colón** (Columbus'

House) was actually built over a hundred years after the explorer's death. Maps of Columbus' various voyages, pieces of Peruvian pottery, and small exhibitions of contemporary Gomeran art are displayed.

Ermita de San Sebastián

MAP P.103
Plaza Hermita 2, San Sebastián. Sporadic opening times, but interesting to view from the outside if closed.

Built in 1450, the tiny **Ermita de San Sebastián** was the island's first chapel but, like most buildings in the town, it was not spared by marauding pirates – they destroyed it no fewer than three times. Recent restoration has returned the building to its original form. The fourteen iron crosses on the wall – among the very few decorations on display in the chapel – represent the Stations of the Cross.

Beatriz de Bobadilla

Playa de San Sebastián and Playa de la Cueva

MAP P.103

San Sebastián

CAFÉ	
Kiosko Ramón	6

RESTAURANTS	
Cuatro Caminos	2
Agape Bistro	5
Junonia	1
Pension Victor	3
La Salamandra	4

ACCOMMODATION	
Parador de la Gomera	2
Torre del Conde	1

BAR	
Blue Marlin Bar	1

Playa de Santiago

San Sebastián's central plazas overlook the sparkling bay, the harbour and a promenade beside the island's longest (400m) sandy beach, **Playa de San Sebastián**. At the eastern end of the promenade, just beyond the marina and through a tunnel, is the town's second, more secluded beach, **Playa de la Cueva**. Also sandy, it's less disturbed by harbour traffic and has great views across to Tenerife and Mount Teide.

Ermita Nuestra Señora de Guadalupe

MAP P.101

A signed path (6.5km/2hr 20min circular) leads from above Playa Ávalo, to the **Ermita Nuestra Señora de Guadeloupe**, a tiny chapel on a promontory north of

Sirope de Palma – the sweet taste of La Gomera

Better known as *miel de Palma* (**palm honey**), the sweet, smoky syrup distilled from the sap of La Gomera's date palms has been a mainstay of island cuisine since before the Spanish conquest. In the *barrancos* of Vallehermoso, the heads of *Phoenix canariensis* (Canarian date palms), which can be 27m (88ft) tall, tower above the dense sub-tropical canopy, their ebullient leaves swaying in the breeze. Standing astride the uppermost leaves at dusk, the *guaraperos* of La Gomera tap the buds of the tree and insert a bamboo chute to collect the sap, or **guarapo**, which rises overnight. Cleaned, filtered and boiled rapidly for two to three hours, the *guarapo* thickens and sweetens to produce the island's famous syrup. Drizzled over goats' cheese, added to salad dressings or used to make traditional desserts such as *leche asada*, this pure, mineral-rich syrup is known as "**the queen of the kitchen**" and you'll find it on menus across the island.

San Sebastián. It's home to a small statue of the Virgin Mary known as the Virgen de Guadalupe, La Gomera's patron saint. Every five years (2018, 2023, etc) on the first Sunday in October, the chapel becomes the focal point of attention in the Fiestas Lustrales, when pilgrims carry the diminutive statue to a fishing boat, which takes her on a tour of the island. Much celebration, singing, dancing and fireworks accompany the tour, finally returning her home on December 12.

Playa de Santiago

MAP P.101

Bus #3 from San Sebastián, Mon–Sat 6 daily, 40min Ⓦ guaguagomera.com/publico/contenido/lineas. Ferries arrive from Valle Gran Rey, 3 daily, 40min; and from San Sebastián, 3 daily, 50min Ⓦ fredolsen.es.

As the Olsen family holiday developments atop the cliff continue to expand, so **Playa de Santiago**'s popularity increases proportionately. To date, limited accommodation at coastal level ensures the village retains its authentic feel, but plans to substantially expand the marina may threaten that if they ever come to fruition. Located in the island's sunniest spot and alongside its airport, the tables and chairs of restaurants sit above the beach looking out over a small harbour and the ocean. Behind the front line, a hotch-potch of white houses huddles around the mouth of the Barranco de Santiago, hemmed in by cliffs.

Where Valle Gran Rey tends to attract predominantly German visitors, you'll hear more English speakers in Playa de Santiago than anywhere else on the island. The beach is mostly pebbly, but it's Santiago's sunny disposition, still-evident fishing village feel and tranquil atmosphere that attract visitors.

Playa de Santiago

CALLE PLAYA SANTIAGO
BARRANCO SANTIAGO
CALLE DE SANTIAGO APÓSTOL
CALLE LES ESCRERAS
CALLE TECINA
CALLE HOTEL
PROL. SANTIAGO APÓSTOL CHART
CALLE DE SANTIAGO APÓSTOL
CALLE LA JUNTA
AVENIDA MARÍTIMA
AVENIDA DEL ALMIRANTE COLÓN
AVENIDA MARÍTIMA
AVENIDA MARÍTIMA
Playa de Santiago
ATLANTIC OCEAN

BAR	
La Chalana	2
CAFÉ	
Tasca-Los Chiko's	3
RESTAURANTS	
Club Laurel	1
La Cuevita	5
Don Tomate	4

ACCOMMODATION	
Apartamentos Tapahuga	2
Jardín Tecina	1

0 metres 200
0 yards 200

Perfect appetisers

Cafés

Kiosko Ramón

MAP P.103
Avda de los Descubridores, San Sebastián ℗ 690 05 59 66. Mon–Sat 5.30am–11.30pm, Sun 8am–8pm.

A hub of local life from the early morning, the greenhouse style design of the building makes it the ideal place for watching the world go by, even when the exterior terrace is a bit on the chilly side. A local-style breakfast of coffee and a tortilla *bocadillo* (baguette) is a great way to start the day.

Tasca Los Chikos

MAP P.105
C/de Santiago Apóstol 94A, Playa de Santiago Ⓦ tascacafeloschikos.wixsite. com. Mon–Sat 8am–10pm.

Tasca Los Chikos is a small family-run coffee shop with a modern vibe. This is a good place to stop for breakfast or a light lunch. A good selection of sandwiches and stuffed croissants are freshly made on site throughout the day. Menu prices are very reasonable for the area, too.

Restaurants

Ágape Bistro

MAP P.103
C/Real 15, San Sebastián Ⓦ agapebistro. com. Tue–Sat 1–11pm.

Jazzy little restaurant in a traditional cottage serving more variety than most others, featuring influences from France and Switzerland as well as Gomera. A small but eclectic menu includes the likes of French parmentier and Swiss fondue, as well as vegetarian options. Reservations are recommended as this is a very small restaurant, with the Swiss chef-owner often working alone and catering for just one or two small groups. ££–£££

Club Laurel

MAP P.105
Hotel Jardin Tecina, Avda del Almirante Colón, Playa de Santiago Ⓦ jardin-tecina. com. Daily 10am–10pm.

Superb beachside setting with shearwaters providing the nightly soundtrack to accompany the classical guitarist. Creative cuisine with fish mains and pizza cooked in the wood-fired oven. Excellent tasting menus including a seven-course, meat-free eco menu. £–££

Cuatro Caminos

MAP P.105
C/Prof. Armas Fernández 1, San Sebastián Ⓦ restaurantecuatrocaminos. com. Mon–Thu 11am–5.m & 7–11pm, Fri 11am–5.30pm & 7–11pm, Sat 11am–5.30pm.

Tucked away in a back street and more popular with locals than visitors, the Canarian cuisine here is better quality than many closer to the seafront. As such, it's a bit more expensive, but the pizzas are cheap and everything is good value, taking into account the quality of the produce. £

La Cuevita

MAP P.105

Avda Marítima, Playa de Santiago ☎ 922 89
55 68. Mon–Sat noon–4pm & 6.30–10pm.
A wide selection of fish and seafood
in a romantically lit cave beside
the harbour. Prices are reasonable
given the setting: garlic tuna, and
cazuela (fish stew) are among the
specialities. £

Don Tomate

MAP P.105
Avda Marítima 56, Playa de Santiago ☎ 922
89 55 45. Tues–Sun noon–4pm & 6–10pm.
Originally an Italian restaurant, the
menu includes fish, meat, pasta and
pizzas. The fish and meat can be on
the expensive side but the pizzas are
good value, with a wide selection of
toppings. £

Junonia

MAP P.105
C/Real 51, San Sebastián ☎ 648 81 01
00. Tue–Fri 6–10pm, Sat noon–10pm, Sun
noon–5pm.
One of the most sophisticated menus
found on La Gomera, this restaurant
serves up a menu of traditional
fish and seafood dishes, including
paella, as well as more contemporary
favourites such as tuna tartare. £

Pension Victor

MAP P.103
C/Real 23, San Sebastián ☎ 922 87 13 35.
Daily noon4pm & 6–10pm, closed Wed.
Quirky restaurant and pension
with an exterior terrace and interior
covered courtyard with hanging
ferns and murals of Gomeran
scenes. The food is nothing
exceptional, just good-value, plain
traditional dishes such as *sopa de
berros* (watercress soup) and tuna
in *mojo*, but it's worth coming here
for the ambience, which is classic
La Gomera – no frills, no fuss. £

La Salamandra

MAP P.103
Pl. de la Constitución 14,San Sebastián
ⓦ lasalamandragastrobar.com. Mon
7–11pm, Tue–Sat 12.30–4pm & 7–11pm.
Boutique restaurant with an
appealing menu. Risotto and pasta

La Salamandra

dishes are good value and although
the steak is relatively pricey, it's
worth every cent and is what keeps
the clientele coming back time and
again. £–££

Bars

Blue Marlin Bar

MAP P.103
Plaza de la Constitución 6, San Sebastián
☎ 922 14 50 65. Mon–Sat 8pm–2am, Sun
8pm–midnight.
Traditionally a sailors' bar, but
now the liveliest venue in town
for cocktails, watching football,
listening to music or just hanging
out with friends.

La Chalana

MAP P.105
Avda del Almirante Colón, Playa de
Santiago ⓦ barlachalana.com. Thurs–Mon
11am–9pm.
Delightfully ramshackle and
eclectic beach bar with a great
soundtrack, set at the eastern edge
of the resort. The most relaxed
venue in town in which to enjoy
drinks, snacks, or lunch with
hypnotic sea views.

Valle Gran Rey

A long, deep *barranco* of stepped terraces punctuated by Canarian palm trees, sweeping down the mountains from the edge of Garajonay to the sea, Valle Gran Rey is impressive to behold and nerve-jangling to drive into. A handful of settlements cling to the valley's sides as it descends to the coast, where it splits into three distinct areas; Vueltas, La Calera and La Playa. A German hippy destination since the 1960s – many of them still live here, hence the proliferation of health food shops and vegetarian restaurants – Valle Gran Rey remains popular with German visitors. The largest resort on La Gomera, it's still quiet and laidback by Tenerife standards.

Vueltas

MAP P.109

At Valle Gran Rey's southern extreme, gaily coloured fishing boats bob in the harbour at **Vueltas** beneath the sheer cliff face; alongside, the small, black-sand Playa de Vueltas shelves slowly into the calm waters, making it a favourite with families. The restaurants that line the harbour are perfect for the gentle art of sitting and people-watching. Clambering up the hillside behind the harbour, a clutch of shops, bars and restaurants line the higgledy-piggledy streets and provide an eclectic after-dark scene.

La Puntilla

MAP P.109

Set in the middle of the long coastal strip is **La Puntilla**, an oversized bronze statue of the Guanche rebel Hautacuperche standing guard over the pretty black-sand beach and rock pools of **Charco del Conde**.

Opposite, holiday apartments accumulate behind a row of bars and restaurants where the laid-back scene morphs into live music after dark, with musicians jamming at some venues.

Argaga tropical fruit garden

MAP P.109

Finca Argaga ☎ 922 69 70 04. Temporarily closed at the time of writing.

The **Argaga tropical fruit garden** (or Tropischer Fruchtgarten) is a fifteen-minute walk south of Vueltas – following first the cliffs opposite the harbour and then a track a short way up the Barranco Argaga (past the "private" signs). Developed by enthusiasts as an organic garden for fruits and flowers, visitor interest has led to the orchard being opened for frequent, pleasantly informal **tours** (in English on request). These concentrate on sampling around a dozen of the exotic fruits grown here, accompanied by salient information on their cultivation.

Arrival and information

Bus #1 from San Sebastián (Mon–Sat 6 daily, Sun 2 daily; 2hr 15min) stops in La Calera, Vueltas and La Playa. **Ferries** (3 daily) from Los Cristianos (1hr 20min) via San Sebastián (35min) and Playa de Santiago (20min) dock at Vueltas. The **tourist office** (Mon–Fri 8am–3pm; ☎ 922 89 56 50, ⓦ lagomera.travel) is in La Playa, behind the promenade.

La Playa, La Puntilla and Vueltas

ACCOMMODATION

Apartamentos Charco del Conde	2
Gran Rey	1
Pension Candelaria	3

SHOPS

El Fotógrafo	1
Mercadillo de Valle Gran Rey	2

BARS

Bar La Tasca	2
Cacatua	3
Gomera Lounge	1

CAFÉ

Bistro-Café Der Anderen Art	5

RESTAURANTS

La Garbanza	3
El Mirador	2
El Puerto	9
Pinocchio	4
Pizzaria Avenida	1
La Salsa	7
Tambara	6
Tuyo	8

LA PLAYA

AV. LA CALERA

VALLE GRAN REY

PLAZA LOMO DEL RIEGO

Bus station

AV. MARITIMA LA PLAYA. LA PUNTILLA

PISTA DEL BALUARTE

C/ DE LAS MALEZAS

CALLEJÓN LA PUNTILLA

C/ LA PLAYA

LA PUNTILLA

BORBALÁN

AV. EL LLANO

C/ EL MANTILLO

N

C/ LA PLAYA

AV. EL LLANO

VUELTAS

C/ VUELTAS

C/ ITALIA

C/ LA HOYA

0	metres	200
0	yards	200

Los Órganos

On the rock face below Vallehermoso, the astonishing **Los Órganos** formations of basaltic columns, rising and falling like the pipes of an organ, were formed by lava cooling and contracting rapidly on contact with the sea, then subjected to the erosive forces of sea and wind. Only visible from the sea, boat trips depart most days – except in rough weather – from Vueltas harbour and take 3–4 hours (including a stop so passengers can have a swim off a small beach only accessible by sea). The trip is provided by Excursiones Tina and Speedy Gomera (Mon, Tue & Thu 9am, Wed 2.30pm, Sun 11am; ⓦ excursiones-tina.com or ⓦ speedy-gomera.com) and you can book in person at the port.

Barranco Argaga hike

MAP P.109
11km, 5hr 30min return, difficult.
Beyond the Argaga tropic fruit garden, the steep, narrow **Barranco Argaga** is an amazing sight and offers great **hiking** – though it's best avoided by anyone who suffers from vertigo. For the fit and brave, there's a 700m ascent over rocky terrain requiring much scrambling and some rock climbing. The start of the route is signposted beyond the fruit orchard and just before the last building at the start of the *barranco* floor. A marked path clambers steeply up Barranco Argaga to the hamlet of Gerián and onto the Ermita de Nuestra Señora de Guadalupe, high on the south slope.

La Playa and Playa del Inglés

MAP P.109
Turn right when you reach the coast at Valle Gran Rey and you'll find yourself in **La Playa**, where nondescript holiday apartments, restaurants and shops clusters around and behind a beach and promenade at the foot of La Merica cliffs. The black-sand beach here is the largest in the resort, and as sunset approaches, crowds begin to gather outside Casa Maria, beer bottle in hand, to watch the sun sink spectacularly into the sea. Being the biggest tourist centre, prices here are noticeably higher than in Vueltas. From La Playa, a dirt track – the only one leading north out of

the village – leads to **Playa del Inglés**, a popular nudist beach.

La Calera and La Merica hike

MAP P.109
5.6km, 4hr one way, difficult.
At the point where the narrow valley opens out towards the sea, a cluster of houses have clawed their way up a cliff to form **La Calera**, the quietest of the main villages in the valley. Here, steep steps and winding alleys connect the old buildings, while above, the magnificent peak **La Merica** offers strenuous **hiking** on rocky trails with tremendous views. A well-trodden track starts from the high road at the up-valley end of La Calera, marked by a large wooden sign, and climbs steeply along a *camino real* with views over to El Hierro on a clear day. You need to be a fit and experienced hiker for this route, and not afraid of heights.

Salto del Agua hike

MAP P.109
3km, 2–3hr return, easy.
This clamber up the rocky, largely dry stream bed of Barranco de Arure leads through dense and atmospheric vegetation to the delightful little waterfall that crashes down the headwall of this minor valley. The **Salto del Agua hike** starts on the inside curve of the sweeping bend in the road just below the village of El Guro; the trailhead is indicated by a sign saying "*Wasserfall*" on a palm tree.

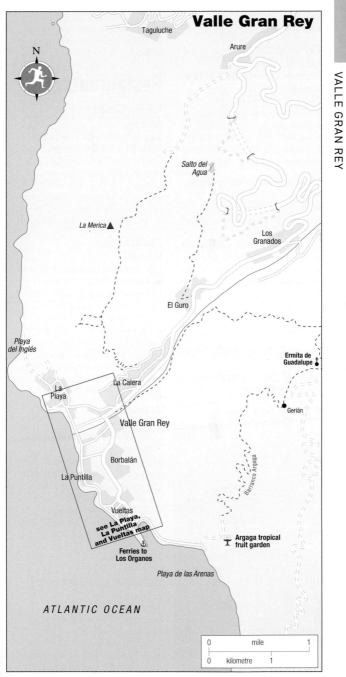

Valle Gran Rey

N

Taguluche

Arure

Salto del Agua

La Merica ▲

Los Granados

El Guro

Playa del Inglés

La Calera

Ermita de Guadalupe

La Playa

Gerián

Valle Gran Rey

Borbalán

La Puntilla

Barranco Argaga

Vueltas

see La Playa, La Puntilla and Vueltas map

Ferries to Los Organos

Argaga tropical fruit garden

Playa de las Arenas

ATLANTIC OCEAN

| 0 | mile | 1 |
| 0 | kilometre | 1 |

Shops

El Fotógrafo

MAP P.109

Promenade, La Playa ☎ 922 80 56 54. Daily 10am–8pm.

Postcards, Gomeran-themed jewellery, T-shirts, hiking maps and guides (most in German) all feature alongside a small fashion collection in this chic boutique. It's also a good place to buy postcards and souvenirs.

Mercadillo de Valle Gran Rey

MAP P.109

Plaza Lomo del Riego (by the bus station), La Calera. Sun 9am–3pm.

Sunday-morning hippy market featuring jewellery, bric-a-brac, clothes and recycled crafts. Expect occasional busking and spontaneous musical performances, too.

Café

Bistro-Café Der Anderen Art

MAP P.109

C/Vueltas 21, Vueltas ☎ 922 80 55 07. Fri–Tue 9am–midnight.

Mercadillo de Valle Gran Rey

Small, friendly café in the centre of town, serving good continental breakfasts, plus cakes and crêpes all day.

Restaurants

La Garbanza

MAP P.109

Lugar la Puntilla ☎ 922 80 54 56. Mon, Tues & Thurs–Sun 5pm–midnight.

The standard of the service can be mixed and it's not cheap, but the Lebanese cuisine is of a very good standard with plenty of choice for vegetarians. A mixed meze platter for two probably the best value. £

El Mirador

MAP P.109

Lugar las Palmitas, La Calera ☎ 922 80 50 86. Mon–Wed & Fri–Sun 1.30–8pm.

Romantic restaurant with a relaxed vibe, located just inland from the coast and on a hillside so there are good sunset views. The food is Canarian cuisine tweaked for more modern tastes with prices a bit higher than more traditional local restaurants. The *menu del día* is a good place to start. £

El Puerto

MAP P.109

C/Vueltas, Vueltas ☎ 922 80 55 30. Daily 1–10pm (closed Wed).

El Puerto is the place to find reasonably priced, good fresh fish and seafood by the harbour in Vueltas – they don't travel far from net to plate. Most seafood dishes, like *lapas* (limpets), are surprisingly cheap given the location. £

Pinocchio

MAP P.109

C/la Playa 44C, La Playa ☎ 922 80 62 97. Wed–Sun 5.30–11pm.

The pizzas cooked in a wood-burning oven (around €8) are excellent, but what's especially appealing about this small restaurant tucked into a cul-de-sac is the after-dark ambience at weekends, when there can be jamming sessions in the street. £

Pizzaria Avenida

MAP P.109

Paseo las Palmeras, La Playa ☎ 922 80 71 15. Mon, Tues & Thurs–Sun 9am–10pm.
Beachside restaurant with nice but pricey tapas. Their pizzas, however, are very good and better value. £

La Salsa

MAP P.109

C/Telémaco 11, Vueltas ☎ 922 80 52 32. Tue–Sat 6–10pm.
The most sophisticated and flavour-packed menu in Valle Gran Rey, with inventive vegetarian options as well as plenty of interesting meat and fish dishes. As a result it's pricier than others, but good value for what you get. £

Tambara

MAP P.109

C/la Cuidadela 12, Vueltas ☎ 922 80 70 95. Wed–Sun 6–11pm.
Occupying a prime sunset dining spot, the tables on the terrace at *Tambara* are in demand but the interior, decorated with Turkish mosaics, is almost as nice anyway. The varied menu includes Canarian cuisine and pasta dishes with a restaurant favourite being couscous with chicken. £

Tuyo

MAP P.109

C/Vueltas 5, Vueltas ⓦ restaurant-tuyo. com. Mon & Thu–Sun 6–11pm
One of the most exciting restaurants on La Gomera, you can feel the influence of the vibrant food scene rubbing off from Tenerife. Asian and Spanish fusion food done to the highest standard. Booking recommended, check the website for guest residences from world-class chefs. £–££

Bars

Bar La Tasca

MAP P.109

C/Cuesta Abisinia 5, Vueltas ⓦ barlatasca. com. Wed–Sun 7pm–midnight.

Canarian limpets

Hidden away in a back street in the Vueltas area, *Bar La Tasca* is lively and mainly attracts locals, and is good for cocktails, live music and watching Champions League football.

Cacatua

MAP P.109

C/Abicinia 5, Vueltas ☎ 922 80 61 04. Mon–Sat 10am–2am.
The most eclectic bar in Valle Gran Rey consists of various rooms and a leafy courtyard patio in and around an old townhouse. The best time to visit is after midnight at weekends, when it buzzes with *canarios*, ex-pats of various nationalities and the occasional visitor who stumbles across it.

Gomera Lounge

MAP P.109

Paseo Las Palmeras 9, La Playa ⓦ gomeralounge.de. Performance times vary, check the website for upcoming events, 8.30–11pm most evenings.
A piano and wine bar which is also something of a cultural meeting point for locals. Regular live music sessions, flamenco and tango performances. There's an appealingly relaxed vibe to the place.

Northern La Gomera

Atlantic trade winds regularly bring clouds and misty rain to northern La Gomera, making its damp, lush valleys the island's most fertile where agriculture is still the mainstay. Here, the ebullient heads of Canarian Date Palms rise above the vegetation and supply the sap from which the island's delicious miel *de Palma* (palm honey) is produced. At the head of these valleys lies the Parque Nacional de Garajonay, a Unesco World Heritage site where lichen hangs from ancient laurel trees in one of the only remaining such forests on the planet. Rugged and unspoiled, this is La Gomera at its best and is superb hiking country – but it's not for the faint hearted.

Hermigua

MAP P.114
Bus #2 from San Sebastián, Mon–Sat 6 daily, Sun 2 daily, 25min; or Vallehermoso, Mon–Sat 6 daily, Sun 2 daily, 45min.

Strung out along the length of a pretty ravine, and fed by water from La Gomera's only stream, **Hermigua** is set in the island's lushest valley, bedecked with the

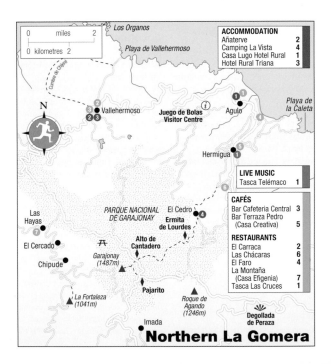

Northern La Gomera

Vallehermoso

torn leaves of banana palms. The town broadly divides into an upper and lower village, the upper marked by the sixteenth-century Iglesia de Santo Domingo while the lower village has a small plaza beside the Nuestra Señora de la Emancipación church with shops, bars, cafés and restaurants lining the road either side and a good-sized supermarket. Where the valley meets the sea is Santa Catalina beach, popular with local surfers but too rough for swimming.

Playa de la Caleta
MAP P.114

Playa de la Caleta lies 6km to the east of Hermigua; it's either a twenty-minute drive or an hour and a half hike over the headland to get there. A pretty, sheltered bay with a good café/restaurant and picnic tables beneath tamarisk trees, the beach is popular with locals and gets very busy on summer weekends and public holidays.

Vallehermoso
MAP P.114
Bus #2 from San Sebastián, Mon–Sat 6 daily, Sun 2 daily, 1hr 10min.

Meaning "beautiful valley", **Vallehermoso** nestles between steep

The legend of Garajonay

The mountain, **Garajonay**, is named after Gomera's answer to Romeo and Juliet, Gara and Jonay. Gara was a Gomeran princess and Jonay a humble peasant boy from Tenerife who visited his princess by paddling over on inflated goatskins – or so the Guanche legend goes. Neither family was keen on the couple's relationship but their love ran far deeper than their differences in status, and so, determined never to be parted, they clambered to the top of Garajonay and ran each other through with lances of laurel wood, choosing death rather than separation and naming the mountain in the process.

ridges below the towering volcanic monolith of Roque Cano and is the best place to base yourself for hiking. The focal point of the village is the Plaza de la Constitución, a small square surrounded by bars, shops, banks and a supermarket. A 3km walk or drive north along Avenida Guillermo Ascanio Moreno, leading to Calle la Playa, takes you to the **beach** and free swimming pool complex with café and sun decks (Tues–Sun, summer only). Head east from the plaza along Calle Poeta Pedro García and just beyond the petrol station you'll arrive at the quirky playground with its giant Alice in Wonderland-style characters also the starting point for a splendid **hike** to Roque Cano (8km, 3hr 30min). South of the village, a pleasant 6km, two-hour hike takes you on a circuit to the lovely Presa La Encantadora reservoir, where you can picnic on its shore.

El Cedro

MAP P.114

Set amid lush cultivated terraces and dense laurel thickets at the northern edge of Garajonay, **El Cedro** is only accessible on foot or by car and is the national park at its best. This modest hamlet makes a good place to stop on longer hikes, with *La Vista* café providing a warm welcome when the mist descends. El Cedro also has an exciting short (roughly 1hr) hike through a claustrophobic 575m underground water tunnel – make sure you bring a torch, expect wet feet and don't undertake it after heavy rains.

Juego de Bolas Visitor Centre

MAP P.114

La Palmita, Agulo ☏ 992 80 09 93. Daily 9.30am–4.30pm. Free.

Located 3km outside the national park, the **Juego de Bolas Visitor Centre** is only accessible by car or by a 2km uphill hike from *Las Rosas* restaurant bus stop. Set around gardens of endemic flora, three display rooms feature extensive information and a video on the park. The **Casa de la Memoria** recreates the interior of a peasant home and holds exhibitions and demonstrations of traditional crafts, including pottery and

El Cedro

Hiking in northern La Gomera

La Gomera is one of the best places in Europe for **winter walking**, with a challenging but rewarding terrain. With multiple trails and eroded sections of paths, you should never set out without detailed walking directions and a map. **Temperatures** can vary wildly, from hot exposed ridges to bone-chilling damp when the *bruma* (low cloud) descends, so dress in layers and bring waterproofs.

GARAJONAY
MAP P.114

5km, 2hr return, moderate. Bus #1 from San Sebastián to Pajarito, Mon–Sat 5 daily, 30min; or Valle Gran Rey, Mon–Sat 5 daily, 1hr 30min.

Superb views over the dense tree canopy and beyond to neighbouring islands – weather permitting. To climb the peak of **Garajonay**, head up from Pajarito in direction marked "Alto de Garajonay 2.5".

ALTO DE CONTADERO TO HERMIGUA
MAP P.114

9km, 4hr one-way, moderate. Bus #1 from San Sebastián to Pajarito, Mon–Sat 5 daily, 30min; or Valle Gran Rey, Mon–Sat 5 daily, 1hr 30min.

Scenically spectacular and wonderfully varied, this is one of the best hikes in La Gomera and is almost entirely downhill. From Pajarito, follow the route to Alto de Garajonay as far as the T-junction, where you turn right for Contadero. When you reach **Alto de Contadero**, follow the trail signposted "El Cedro 4.8". Beyond El Cedro, the path descends steeply back into **Hermigua**.

CUMBRE DE CHIJERÉ
MAP P.114

10km, 4hr return, moderate to difficult. Bus #2 from San Sebastián, Mon–Sat 6 daily, Sun 2 daily, 1hr 10min.

A beautiful ridge walk starting from Vallehermoso where a path ascends a steep-sided gorge a few hundred metres shy of the beach. The trail zigzags its way up the arid, rocky slopes, with views of rugged cliffs and Teide on Tenerife in the distance, to reach the top of the **Cumbre de Chijeré** ridge. A dirt path then snakes its way along the ridge, passing a couple of chapels, before descending back into the centre of Vallehermoso.

LA FORTALEZA
MAP P.114

5km, 2hr return, moderate to difficult. Bus #1 from Valle Gran Rey, Mon–Sat 6 daily, Sun 2 daily, 45min; or from San Sebastián, Mon–Sat 6 daily, Sun 2 daily, 1hr.

Starting out along the road south from Chipude to La Dama, follow the track up the hill to the left of the road to reach the summit plateau of **La Fortaleza** – this definitely isn't one for vertigo sufferers. For Guanches, this was an important place of retreat and worship and remains of stone circles have been found here, along with bone fragments from goats and sheep, suggesting sacrifices.

weaving. There's a small café and a shop where you can buy artisan produce, too.

Mirador de Abrante

MAP P.114
Ctra del Mirador, La Palmita, Agulo ☎ 922 14 60 00. Daily: June–Sept 11am–7pm; Oct–May 10am–6pm. Free.

Viewpoint on the top of the Abrante cliffs with a glass skywalk suspended 625m above sea level, offering views over Agulo and towards Mount Teide. The **Mirador de Abrante** is a 1.6km walk from Juego de Bolas – follow signs to Agulo and then to Mirador.

Agulo

MAP P.114
Bus #2 from San Sebastián. Mon–Sat 6 daily, Sun 2 daily, 20min.

Huddled on a tight shelf above the sea, charming seventeenth-century **Agulo** is La Gomera's best-preserved traditional village and is considered its prettiest. Its maze of cobbled alleys and whitewashed houses are clustered at the foot of the mountains, hemmed in by the Las Rosas and Lepe *barrancos*. After winter rains, waterfalls cascade down the cliff face and on the **Eve of San Marcos** (April 24), local youths jump over juniper wood bonfires.

Chipude and El Cercado

MAP P.114
Chipude: Bus #1 Mon–Sat 6 daily, Sun 2 daily, from Valle Gran Rey (45min) or from San Sebastián (1hr). El Cercado: ☎ 922 80 41 04, ⓦ vallehermosoweb.es.

The island's oldest settlement, and once its largest town, only the sixteenth-century Moorish Iglesia de la Virgen de la Candelaria hints at the bygone importance of **Chipude**. The village is overseen by the imposing grandeur of La Fortaleza, the tabletop mountain held sacred by the Guanche. Located just 2km west of Chipude, the hamlet of **El Cercado** is known for its traditional pottery thrown by hand and finished in a red earth glaze. Visit **Centro de Interpretación las Loceras museum** (Tue–Sun 11am–3pm; free) in the village to learn more about the pottery, and the women who keep the craft alive.

Agulo

Cafés

Bar Cafeteria Central

MAP P.114

Plaza de la Constitución, Vallehermoso
☎ 922 80 00 23. Mon–Sat 6am–10pm.

Occupying a sunny corner of the main square, this is the place in town to get to know some very local tipples like *Gomerón* (palm honey and aguardiente) or aromatic *mistela* (wine, orange peel, cinnamon, cloves and aniseed). Also serves good coffee and pastries.

Bar Terraza Pedro (Casa Creativa)

MAP P.114

Ctra General 154, Hermigua
ⓦ barterrazapedro.com. Tue–Sun 9am–11pm.

A meeting point for locals and a popular post-walk refreshment stop for hikers, with views over the banana plantations and surrounding hills. Still known by its former name, *Casa Creativa*, it's friendly and relaxed, and the music is good.

Restaurants

El Carraca

MAP P.114

C/Nueva Creacion, Vallehermoso ☎ 922 780 10 21. Tues–Thu & Sun 8am–11pm, Fri & Sat 8am–midnight.

Attractive restaurant and bar with a menu featuring local favourites. A cut above many traditional restaurants; soup is served with a bowl of *gofio* (toasted flour) and the *almogrote* (cheese pâté) comes with mini toasts. £

Las Chácaras

MAP P.114

C/Cabo 2, Hermigua ⓦ laschacaras.com. Mon–Sat 9am–11.30pm.

The menu has a wide selection of traditional dishes such as *potaje de berros* (watercress soup) and *cabra* (goat); owner César claims he makes the spiciest *mojos* (sauces) in the Canaries (available to take away). £

El Faro

MAP P.114

Ctra Playa 15, Hermigua ☎ 922 88 00 62. Mon, Tues & Thurs–Sun 1–10pm.

Fish and seafood is what *El Faro* does best. If the weather's good, head to the panoramic terrace overlooking Santa Catalina beach. Fish dishes are the star of the show, but meat and vegetarian options are available. £

La Montaña (Casa Efigenia)

MAP P.114

Plaza de los Eucaliptos, Las Hayas ⓦ efigenianatural.com. Daily 8am–8pm (closed Tue).

A vegetarian restaurant in the woods, eating at *Casa Efigenia* is a uniquely La Gomera experience. The delicious set menu of salad, *puchero* (stew), *almogrote* and dessert features home-grown ingredients and hasn't changed in years, and for good reason – it is very popular. £

Tasca las Cruces

MAP P.114

C/Pedro Bethencourt 15B, Agulo ☎ 666 24 77 47. Tue 6.30–10.30pm, Wed–Sat noon–4.30pm & 6.30–10.30pm, Sun noon–4.30pm.

Local favourite with plenty of outdoor seating, making this a great place to people-watch and observe daily life in a typical Canarian town. The food is traditional and reasonably priced, with generous portions, as you would expect of somewhere catering mainly to locals. £

Live music

Tasca Telémaco

MAP P.114

Plaza de la de la Encarnación 2, Hermigua ⓦ tascatelemaco.com. Daily (except Tue) 1–3pm & 6.30–10pm.

An excellent restaurant serving a fusion of local, international and vegetarian dishes, *Tasca Telémaco* is also a venue for eclectic entertainment. Events include concerts, themed nights (*fiesta del sombrero*) and even fashion shows. ££

ACCOMMODATION

Europe Villa Cortes

Accommodation

Tenerife's accommodation choices are dominated by the hotel sector, with exponential growth in the luxury market over the last decade or so. The majority of visitors stay in the three- and four-star hotels and aparthotels (apartments within hotel complexes) which populate resorts. For a more authentic experience, head to one of the rural hotels and houses (*hoteles rurales* and *casas rurales*), traditional homes ranging from rustic to chic. Self-catering on both Tenerife and La Gomera offers the best value for money and there are plenty of choices on the likes of ⓦairbnb.com and ⓦbooking.com. Pensions are more common in the north of Tenerife than the south, and even then, they're not present in big numbers. The same is true of hostels, which tend to be outside of main resorts and are not widespread on either island. There's a handful of campsites with on-site facilities, but they don't tend to be in attractive locations and many don't even allow you to pitch your own tent. A better choice is camping wild at a *zona recreativa* (picnic zone), where you can pitch up for free – but you do need prior permission and your own tent (see ⓦcentralreservas.tenerife.es for details). High season on Tenerife and La Gomera, when prices are highest, is January to Easter; prices below are for the cheapest double room in these months. Consider visiting during the shoulder seasons of May and September/October for best value.

Santa Cruz

IBEROSTAR HERITAGE GRAND MENCEY MAP P.28 POCKET MAP C1. C/Doctor José Naveiras 38 ⓦiberostar.com. Contemporary chic blends beautifully with colonial elegance and a leafy location in *Iberostar Grand Hotel Mencey*, the city's only five-star hotel. The high ceilings add a feeling of luxury. ££

DREAM APARTMENTS MAP P.28 POCKET MAP C2. C/San Nicolas 4, ⓦdreamapartmentscanarias.com. Fully equipped apartments with kitchen and washing machine. Santa Cruz is probably the best place on the island for self-catering, thanks to the abundance of grocery stores and takeaway restaurants near at hand. See the website for other properties across Tenerife. £

OCCIDENTAL SANTA CRUZ CONTEMPORÁNEO MAP P.28 POCKET MAP C1. Rambla de Santa Cruz 116 ⓦbarcelo.com. Stylish modernism, a good breakfast and great value for money in this chic hotel alongside Parque García Sanabria. £

SILKEN ATLÁNTIDA MAP P.28 POCKET MAP B5. Avda Tres de Mayo 3 ⓦhoteles-silken.com. Good-sized rooms and great city views from the lift and rooftop terrace in this glass-and-chrome hotel, nicely located for shopping malls and the

Auditorium. Breakfast not included. £

La Laguna and the Anaga

AGUERE MAP P.37 C/Obispo Rey Redondo 55 Ⓦ hotelaguere.es. This converted eighteenth-century manor house on a pedestrianised street in the heart of the city has basic but clean and comfortable rooms surrounding an attractive inner courtyard. Breakfast is served in the courtyard café. ££

ALBERGUE MONTES DE ANAGA MAP P.37 Ctra Bailadero–Chamorga s/n Ⓦ alberguestenerife.net. A mountain hostel on a ridge on the Chamorga road in the heart of the Anaga, with magnificent hiking straight from the door. Popular with groups. Dorms and private rooms available. ££

CASA RURAL LA ASOMADA DEL GATO MAP P.37 C/Anchieta 45 Ⓦ laasomadadelgato.es. Small and simple hotel, but centrally located for exploring the town. Rooms are not luxurious, but they are comfortable and clean, and the owners are very welcoming. £

COSTA SALADA HOTEL RURAL MAP P.37 Ctra de la Costa, Valle Guerra Ⓦ costasalada.es. Lovely, family-run, rural boutique hotel set within a lovely plants *finca* in humid Valle de Guerra. On the headland with views over the Anaga mountains, gardens tumble down to a swimming pool above the ocean. ££

NIVARIA MAP P.37 Plaza del Adelantado 11 Ⓦ lagunanivaria.com. A beautiful sixteenth-century manor house set on the city's main plaza, this boutique hotel blends colonial style with contemporary comfort. Rooms are more spacious than the average city-centre hotel, and breakfast is excellent. The hotel also has a spa and gym. ££

Candelaria and Güímar

FINCA SALAMANCA MAP P.50 Ctra Güímar, El Puertito 2, Güímar Ⓦ hotelfincasalamanca.com. Set on an avocado plantation within walking distance of El Puertito, this genteel rural hotel is nestled among extensive botanical gardens and has an elegant swimming pool and a good, on-site restaurant. £–££

Puerto de la Cruz and around

ALHAMBRA MAP P.54 C/Nicandro Gonzales Borges 19 Ⓦ alhambra-orotava. com. Uniquely styled villa with elaborate Moorish décor, generous floor space and sumptuous en suites. A short walk from Plaza de la Constitución, there are six, individually styled double rooms. Facilities include a pool and sauna. ££

BOTÁNICO MAP P.50 C/Richard J Yeoward 1 Ⓦ hotelbotanico.com. Thai-style decor, splendid botanical gardens and an award-winning spa: this is a grand dame of a hotel, alongside the Jardines Botanicos (see page 53). Although immaculate, rooms feel old-fashioned – but luckily the customer service is impeccably old school, too, putting this hotel firmly in the five-star category. £££

CASABLANCA MAP P.50 Calzada de Martiánez 4 Ⓦ apartamentosclubcasablanca.com. Great value for money in these spacious, modern and well-equipped studios and one- and two-bedroom apartments in the La Paz district, an uphill walk home from beaches and town centre. Minimum two-night stay in high season. £

HOTEL RURAL VICTORIA MAP P.54 C/ Hermano Apolinar 8 Ⓦ hotelruralvictoria. com. Rural hotel in the centre of La Orotava, close to Victoria Gardens and Casa de los Balcones. The balconied interior courtyard has original tiling, plus there's an excellent restaurant and great views from the roof terrace. £

MONOPOL MAP P.50 C/Quintana 15 Ⓦ monopoltf.com. This eighteenth-century colonial hotel occupies an unbeatable position opposite Plaza de la Iglesia – try for one of the rooms overlooking it. Decor is tired and rooms are basic but service is warm and friendly. £

PUERTO AZUL MAP P.50 C/Lomo 24 ⓦ puerto-azul.com. Small, basic hotel in the *Ranilla* (restaurant) district. More like a hostel, the rooms are cheap but are in need of refurbishment, but the warm welcome and reasonable rates go some way towards making up for lack of quality. **£**

RIU GAROE MAP P.50 C/Doctor Celestino Gonzalez Padron 3 ⓦ riu.com. Traditional Canarian hotel in the La Paz district, a 25min walk from beaches and town centre. Favoured by a more mature clientele, rooms are in low-rise blocks with wooden balconies, set around expansive gardens. It also has separate adult and child swimming pools. **££**

TIGAIGA MAP P.50 Parque Taoro 28 ⓦ tigaiga.com. Award-winning service in this family-run hotel set among extensive, palm-filled gardens above the town and alongside Parque Taoro. Warm, friendly and efficient service and tranquil, leafy surroundings keep guests returning year after year. Minimum two nights' stay in high season. **££**

Garachico and the Teno

HACIENDA DEL CONDE MAP P.62 El C/ Finca, Buenavista del Norte ⓦ melia. com. Adults-only boutique spa hotel in contemporary colonial style, set on the remote northeast coast alongside a golf course. The perfect de-stress getaway for those seeking an alternative side to Tenerife, and with no budget constraints. **£££**

EL PATIO MAP P.62 Finca Malpais, El Guincho ⓦ hotelpatio.com. Sixteenth-century rural hotel set in a sea of bananas on the lush north west coast, a five minute drive from Garachico. Period furniture, traditional architecture and a palm-filled patio accompany the tranquillity. Minimum three nights' stay in high season. **££**

SAN ROQUE MAP P.62 C/Esteban Ponte 32 ⓦ hotelsanroque.com. The best rural hotel on the island, this impeccably renovated eighteenth-century manor house combines traditional features with Bauhaus styling and Rennie Mackintosh furniture – a surprising mixture, but it works. Adults

only; breakfast not included. **£££**

TREVEJO YOUTH HOSTEL MAP P.62 C/ Francisco Martínez de Fuentes 5 ☎ 676 96 41 85. Clean, contemporary hostel in the centre of Garachico, close to Plaza de la Libertad. Accommodation is bunk beds in three, en suite dormitories and there's a shared kitchen, lounge and small terrace. Breakfast not included. **Dorms £**

The west coast

BARCELÓ SANTIAGO MAP P.86 C/La Hondura 8, Puerto Santiago ⓦ barcelo. com. Set in a busy resort area with jaw-dropping views over the cliffs of Los Gigantes and sunsets over La Gomera, this friendly hotel centres on vast infinity pools and sun terraces. Popular with families; breakfast not included. **££**

LA CASONA DEL PATIO MAP P.86 Avda de la Iglesia, Santiago del Teide ⓦ ginestarhotels.com. Boutique, rural hotel set in the quiet village of Santiago del Teide with good access to walking and to Masca. Rooms are all individually styled and there's a small spa that you can hire by the hour. **££**

GRAN MELIA PALACIO DE ISORA MAP P.86 Avda los Océanos, Alcalá ⓦ melia. com. This hip, palatial hotel expands across the headland east of the village of Alcalá and offers a plethora of deluxe features, including the longest salt water hotel infinity pool in Europe and a luxury spa . **£££**

POBLADO MARINERO MAP P.86 C/Guios, Los Gigantes ⓦ pobladomarinero.com. Canarian village-style apartment complex beside Los Gigantes' marina and beach, with free access to El Laguillo swimming pool complex. The one- and two- bedroom apartments have a kitchen, bathroom and lounge. **£**

RITZ CARLTON ABAMA MAP P.86 C/ General km9, Guia de Isora ⓦ ritzcarlton. com. Opulent, Moroccan-style mega hotel with its own championship golf course, set atop the cliffs above Playa de San Juan. Considered one of the best hotels in Tenerife, two of its restaurants have Michelin stars, its beach is golden and the sunsets are stunning. £££

The southwest resorts

ANDREA'S MAP P.74 Avda Valle Menéndez 6, Los Cristianos W hotel-andreas.com. Basic budget hotel, well positioned for an early ferry to La Gomera. Rooms are clean and comfortable. Breakfast not included. £

BAHIA DEL DUQUE MAP P.77 Avda de Bruselas W thetaishotels.com. The forerunner of Tenerife's love affair with luxury hotels, the mock-Canarian style of the Del Duque once dominated Costa Adeje. Others have since emulated its opulence, but it remains one of the island's best – and priciest – hotels. The onsite restaurant is the new home of Michelin-starred Nub. £££

COLÓN GUANAHANI MAP P.77 Avda de Bruselas, Costa Adeje W hotelcolonguanahani.com. Soft pastel colours and bleached wood in the rooms give this adults-only hotel a Hamptons-meets-Tenerife style. There's a pretty courtyard pool and it's a 5min stroll to the beach. ££

EUROPE VILLA CORTES MAP P.74 Avda Rafael Puig Lluvina 38, Playa de Las Américas W europe-hotels.org. Authentic Mexican-hacienda style, gourmet food and superb grounds featuring Ibero-American artefacts add character to this sumptuous hotel in the heart of the resort. With its own private beach and a luxurious spa. Rooms ooze old-fashioned luxury. £££

GRAN COSTA ADEJE MAP P.77 Avda de Bruselas 16, Costa Adeje W gfhoteles. com. Perennially popular hotel, favoured by families on all-inclusive trips. This is indisputably a five-star joint but its quality lags behind its more contemporary peers. The friendly service and excellent value for money more than make up for that though. ££

HARD ROCK HOTEL MAP P.74 Avda de Adeje 300, Playa Paraíso W hardrockhotel. com. Tenerife's hippest addition to its deluxe hotel stable, *Hard Rock* has all the trademark pizazz of the Brand. It's all housed in twin towers – one is adults-only – set in capacious grounds, including a beach club/concert venue. ££

PARQUE SANTIAGO III & IV MAP P.74 Avda Las Américas, Playa de Las Américas W parquesantiagotenerife.com. Two stylish, low-rise apartment complexes on the Playa de Las Américas coastline. The high quality one- to four-bedroom apartments and villas are set around courtyard swimming pools and sun terraces. ££

SENSIMAR ARONA GRAN MAP P.74 Avda Juan Carlos 1, Los Cristianos W springhoteles.com. Ferns cascade down four storeys of the cavernous, open-plan lobby of this genteel adults-only spa hotel set at the southern extreme of the resort. Swimming pools and sun terraces abound. Popular with mature guests; adults only. ££

LA TORTUGA HOSTEL MAP P.77 C/Reykjavik, Costa Adeje 52, W latortugahostel.com. Trendy, contemporary hostel in one of the most upmarket areas of Costa Adeje, with shared and private rooms. Fully equipped kitchen, large lounge, dining room and lovely garden with a small pool and covered terrace. £

The southeast coast

VILLA 8 ISLAS MAP P.86 C/Garañaña, Costa del Silencio W villa8islas.com. Smart guest house with eight rooms, each themed around one of the Canary Islands. There is also use of a shared kitchen with allocated space for each room. Outside there is a garden with fruit trees to relax under, as well as an indoor TV and games room. Not all rooms are en suite, check when booking. Bicycle hire available. £

CAMPING LA NAUTA MAP P.86 Ctra General 6225, km 1.5, off the road to Guaza W campingnauta.es. In an isolated position on a hot, breezy and dusty site mostly given over to wooden cabins (sleeping up to 4 people), *La Nauta* is popular with large groups. Facilities include swimming pool, café and sports area. Various options available, including tents, camper vans and cabins. £

CAMPING MONTAÑA ROJA MAP P.86
On TF-643 between El Médano and Los
Abrigos ⓦ campingmontanaroja.com.
Wooden cabañas (sleeping 1–4 people),
mobile homes and tent pitches on a large
site behind El Médano's loveliest beach, La
Tejita. Also has a decent on-site café and
restaurant. **Camping and cabañas £**

PLAYA SUR TENERIFE MAP P.86 C/
Gaviota 36, El Médano ⓦ hotelplayasur.
com. Behind Playa El Médano, at the end
of the boardwalk, so close to the beach
that sand gets into its corridors. Jaded and
faded, it's mainly surfers, groups and those
with early flights who stay here. **££**

Teide and the interior

ALTA MONTAÑA MAP P.92 C/Morro
del Cano 1, Vilaflor ⓦ hotelaltamontana.
com. Just outside the centre of Vilaflor,
this friendly rural hotel has bright, modern,
chalet-style rooms, a garden with a small
swimming pool, and splendid coastal views.
An ideal base for exploring Parque Nacional
del Teide. **£**

HOTEL SPA VILLALBA MAP P.92 C/San
Roque, Vilaflor ⓦ hotelvillalba.com. Adult-
only, eco-conscious rural boutique hotel on
the edge of the pine forest above Vilaflor.
Use of the spa is included in room rates.
Good food along with wine from the family's
own *bodega*. **££**

PARADOR DE LAS CAÑADAS DEL TEIDE
MAP P.92 Las Cañadas del Teide
ⓦ parador.es. The only accommodation in
Parque National del Teide, you're unlikely
ever to have stayed in such a unique
location. Self-styled as a 'mountain lodge',
the location is exceptional and lounging in
the outdoor pool feels very special when
excellent food, friendly staff and starry,
starry nights at the foot of the volcano. **££**

San Sebastián and southern La Gomera

APARTAMENTOS TAPAHUGA MAP P.105
Avda Maritima 52, Playa de Santiago
ⓦ tapahuga.es. Immaculately maintained,
one-bedroom apartments on the promenade

in the heart of the village alongside beach
and restaurants, with a rooftop pool and
solarium. **£**

JARDÍN TECINA MAP P.105 Playa de
Santiago ⓦ jardin-tecina.com. Canarian
village-styled resort with over 400 rooms,
including family suites, and five swimming
pools, set around opulent botanical
gardens. Perched on the clifftop above
the village alongside a championship golf
course, a lift inside the cliff takes guests to
beach level. **£££**

PARADOR DE LA GOMERA MAP P.103
Lomo de la Horca, San Sebastián
ⓦ parador.es. Built in traditional Canarian
style, it's the stunning clifftop position
and magnificent botanical gardens that
give La Gomera's *parador* its leading edge.
Both the food and the service, though, can
sometimes be below par for the price. **£££**

TORRE DEL CONDE MAP P.103 C/Ruíz de
Padrón 17, San Sebastián ☎ 922 87 00
00, ⓦ hoteltorredelconde.com. Centrally
located overlooking the park and Torre del
Condé (see page 100), rooms are basic and
decor is outdated but the service is friendly.
There's a rooftop terrace with sun loungers,
whirlpool tub and nudist zone. **€75**

Valle Gran Rey

APARTAMENTOS CHARCO DEL CONDE
MAP P.111 Marítima Charco de Conde
7 ⓦ charcodelconde.com. Two-storey
apartment block opposite Charco del Conde.
Refurbished in 2021. Apartments have one
bedroom, kitchen, lounge area and either
sea or swimming pool views. There is also a
rooftop sun terrace with views out to sea. **£**

GRAN REY MAP P.111 Avenida Marítima
ⓦ hotelgranrey.es. The only hotel
occupying a frontline position in the resort,
the Gran Rey's decor is a little faded
nowadays and its clientele a tad mature but
its eco-conscious practices, tennis court
and rooftop pool and restaurant keep it in
the running. **££**

PENSION CANDELARIA MAP P.111 C/
Italia 18, Vueltas ⓦ pensioncandelaria.
com. Family-run pension in the village of

Vueltas, a 5min walk from the beach. Nicely appointed and well maintained, the studios and apartments share a lovely roof terrace with sun loungers and ocean views. **£**

Northern La Gomera

AÑATERVE MAP P.114 C/Rodadera, Vallehermoso Ⓦ anaterve.com. Small, friendly rural hotel in a former barracks set high above the village with panoramic views from the roof terrace. It has been beautifully restored by Dutch owners Amala and Herman, who treat all guests like friends. **£**

CAMPING LA VISTA MAP P.114 El Cedro Ⓦ camping-lavista.jimdo.com. La Gomera's only campsite, and the only place you can legally pitch in Parque Nacional de Garajonay, *La Vista* is a very small site, located 800m above sea level in the midst of natural beauty. The restaurant alongside provides good, hearty meals. **£**

CASA LUGO HOTEL RURAL MAP P.114 C/ Pintor Aguiar 33, Agulo Ⓣ 922 14 61 30. Beautifully restored manor house in the picturesque village of Agulo. From wooden floors and window seats to enclosed balcony and open courtyard, original features abound. Bicycle rental available. **£**

HOTEL RURAL TRIANA MAP P.114 C/Triana 30, Vallehermoso Ⓦ hotelruraltriana.es. Rooms are basic and could do with modernisation, but the central location is hard to beat for exploring Vallehermoso. The setting fits nicely with the no-nonsense charm of La Gomera and the local owners are extremely knowledgeable about the area and can direct you to beautiful walks in the surrounding countryside. **£**

ESSENTIALS

Carnival in Santa Cruz

Arrival

Tenerife

By air

The majority of international flights land at **Tenerife South Airport** (Reina Sofía; ☏ 902 404 704, ⊕ aena.es), most arriving from European destinations – there are flights from over twenty UK and Irish cities alone. **Tenerife North** (Los Rodeos; ☏ 922 63 56 35, ⊕ aena.es) handles mainly inter-island routes and flights to the Spanish mainland. While many holidaymakers have **hotel transfers** included in their package, for those travelling independently there are taxis, private shuttle services and frequent public buses running from airports to major towns.

By bus

The #111 bus connects Tenerife South airport with Santa Cruz (1hr), Los Cristianos (25min) and Costa Adeje (35min). It runs every 30 mins throughout the day to Costa Adeje and Santa Cruz. The #343 runs between the airport and Puerto de la Cruz (1hr 25min) eleven times daily.

The #343 runs from Tenerife North airport to Puerto de la Cruz (40min) eleven times a day; its southbound service travels instead to Los Cristianos (1hr 25min), twelve times daily. The #102 service runs from the airport to Santa Cruz (30min) and Puerto de la Cruz (35min) approx thirty times daily. The #107 travels via the airport between Santa Cruz and Buenavista del Norte four times daily, while the #108 connects the airport with Santa Cruz and Icod de los Vinos six times daily.

La Gomera

By air

La Gomera's airport has no international flights, the only route being between the island and Tenerife Norte. For many visitors the most practical option is instead to fly to Tenerife and take a ferry from Los Cristianos to San Sebastián.

By ferry

Two **ferry** companies sail from Los Cristianos to La Gomera: **Fred Olsen** (☏ 902 10 01 07, ⊕ fredolsen.es; 3 daily to San Sebastián, 50min) and **Naviera Armas** (☏ 902 45 65 00, ⊕ navieraarmas.com; 2–3 daily to San Sebastián, 1hr; 2 daily to Valle Gran Rey, 2hr).

Fred Olsen's *Benchi Express* usually sails from San Sebastián to Playa de Santiago and Valle Gran Rey three times daily. (This service was not operational at the time of writing, check online).

Getting around

Tenerife has an excellent public **bus** service and **taxis** are reasonably priced. For getting off the beaten track, **renting a car** is practical and inexpensive. Getting around La Gomera is more difficult: the bus network is skeletal, making renting a car preferable. **Coach** excursions remain popular and widely advertised in hotels and travel agents in resorts.

Buses

Tenerife buses are called *guaguas* (pronounced *wah-wahs*); **TITSA** (⊕ titsa.com) offers an inexpensive service covering most of the island. Fares are low – Los Cristianos to Tenerife South airport costs €2.20 – and can be reduced further by using a **Bono card** (€15 and €25), available only on Tenerife. They can be bought at bus stations and some newsagents and are valid on all routes except those to Mount Teide.

There are reduced services on weekends and fiestas. **Timetables** (*horarios*) are available from bus stations, some kiosks and tourist information centres. Alternatively, use the TITSA website to plan journeys.

La Gomera has seven routes, operated by **Guagua Gomera** (ⓦguaguagomera.com): Line 1 covers Valle Gran Rey–San Sebastián; Line 2 Vallehermoso–San Sebastián; Line 3 Alajeró–San Sebastián; Line 4 Vallehermoso–La Dama; Line 5 Vallehermoso–Alojera; Line 6 airport–Valle Gran Rey; Line 7 airport–San Sebastián. Services are infrequent, but with tickets costing €2–6 they're a cheap way to travel around the island.

Taxis

Taxi ranks in major towns and resorts are generally easy to find. The minimum charge is €3.15, with surcharges added for luggage, travel between 10pm and 6am or on Sundays, and journeys to the airports. Hired for **excursions**, taxis can be cost effective if there are several of you to split the cost. Approximate fares are displayed at some ranks and can be checked at ⓦofficialtaxitenerife.com.

By car

Car rental on Tenerife is inexpensive and practical for exploring areas poorly served by the bus network. Country roads can be twisting and tiring to drive but are relatively quiet. The **Anillo Insular**, a new wide road connecting the northwest and southwest coasts, has made a significant difference to the time it takes to drive across the west of Tenerife. In cities and bigger towns driving can be a hectic experience, and finding a parking space in the street is often tricky. Heading to the nearest pay-and-display car park is usually the best option; they are well-signed.

To rent a car you generally need to be **over 21** (some operators won't rent to under-25s) and to have had a licence for over a year. EU **licences** are accepted as are most foreign licences, though it is recommended these are accompanied by an International Driving Permit. Most operators require a credit-card number. **Rates** start at around €20–30 per day, with discounts for rentals of a week or more. Rental usually includes tax, unlimited mileage and full insurance, but details should be double-checked with rental firms. Most companies won't allow you to island hop with them.

Taxi companies

Las Américas ☎ 922 71 54 07, or from the ranks on the main seafront road.
Candelaria ☎ 922 50 01 90.
Los Cristianos ☎ 922 79 54 14, or from beside the Plaza del Carmen.
Las Galletas ☎ 922 39 09 24.
Garachico ☎ 922 83 00 56.
Güimar ☎ 922 51 08 11.
Icod de Los Vinos ☎ 922 81 08 95.
Puerto de la Cruz ☎ 922 38 58 18, or at the main rank beside Plaza del Charco.
San Sebastián ☎ 922 87 05 24, or at the harbour beside Plaza de las Américas.
Santa Cruz ☎ 922 64 11 22, or at the main rank in Plaza de España.

Car rental companies

AutoReisen Tenerife South airport ☎ 922 39 22 16, Tenerife North airport ☎ 922 26 22 02, ⊛ autoreisen.com.

Avis Tenerife North and South airports ☎ 902 51 15 20, ⊛ avis.es.

Cicar Tenerife North and South airports and La Gomera airport ☎ 928 82 29 00, ⊛ cicar.com.

Hertz Tenerife South Airport ☎ 922 75 93 19, Tenerife North airport ☎ 922 63 58 68, ⊛ hertz.com.

Pluscar Tenerife South airport ☎ 922 70 39 65, Tenerife North airport ☎ 922 89 43 53, ⊛ pluscar-tenerife.com.

La Rueda La Gomera, San Sebastián ☎ 922 87 20 48, Valle Gran Rey ☎ 922 80 51 97, ⊛ autoslarueda.es.

Piñero La Gomera, San Sebastián ☎ 922 87 22 26, ⊛ rentacarpinero.com.

Tours

Tenerife bus tours include excursions around the island as well as itineraries that typically go to Masca and the Parque Nacional del Teide, or Santa Cruz and the Anaga. **Prices** range from €20 to €30; day trips to La Gomera are between €55 and €70. Research reviews online before booking – there are plenty of companies to choose from.

Sports and leisure

Tenerife and La Gomera offer a great range of sea- and land-based activities, most of which are possible year-round thanks to the archipelago's consistently fine weather.

Surfing and bodyboarding

The heavy seas all around Tenerife attract thrill-seeking local surfers and bodyboarders in droves, while visitors tend to head to **Playa de Troya** in Las Américas. Near to the beach in Centro Commercial Américas, the K-16 surf shop (C/México 47, ☎ 922 78 87 79, ⊛ k16surfschooltenerife.com) offers gear rental and instruction for all levels from €40.

Windsurfing and kitesurfing

El Médano is renowned as premium windsurfing and kitesurfing territory, with international competitions regularly held here. Both equipment hire and lessons are available from a number of outlets in the town including 30 Nudos (Paseo Mercedes de la Roja 24, ☎ 922 17 89 05, ⊛ 30nudos.com) and Red Rock Surf & Kite Academy (Paseo Mercedes de la Roja 34, ☎ 922 07 60 94, ⊛ redrocksurf. com). Lessons start from around €45.

Snorkelling and scuba diving

Some of the more sheltered shores of both islands are suitable for snorkelling and there's scuba diving at a number of good sites including the spectacular underwater cliffs just south of **Los Cristianos**, the so-called Stingray City near **Las Galletas**, and a DC3 plane wreck near **Puerto de la Cruz**.

Boat trips, deep-sea fishing and sailing

Boat trips are on offer from Las Américas, Los Cristianos and Los Gigantes. Some are specifically **fishing trips** (from around €65 for half a day), with deep-sea fishing for tuna, swordfish, mako and dorado especially popular. **Chartering** of

Hiking companies

Tenerife Tenerife Guided Walks ☏ 616 89 29 09, ⊕ tenerife-guided-walks.com.
La Gomera Gomera Guide ☏ 636 68 10 86, ⊕ gomeraguide.com.

boats is available from Puerto Colón, Playa de las Américas. Tenerife Sailing Charters (☏ 627 06 99 12, ⊕ tenerifesailingcharters.com), charges around €550 for three hours on a yacht carrying up to eleven people.

Hiking

Puerto de la Cruz is traditionally Tenerife's resort of choice for hikers. It's well connected by buses, has a good range of accommodation, and is on the north side of the island, where the best hiking is to be found. **Santa Cruz** and **La Laguna** can also make good bases, particularly for access to the Anaga. Free maps and hiking guides are available at tourist offices, but are notoriously vague and out of date. Detailed **walking guides** are available from Sunflower Guides (⊕ sunflowerbooks.co.uk), Discovery Walking Guides (⊕ dwgwalking.co.uk) and Cicerone (⊕ cicerone.co.uk) for

both Tenerife and La Gomera, and Walking Tenerife (⊕ walkingtenerife.co.uk) has downloadable PDFs as well as a print guide. The best maps for hikers are from Kompass (available to buy on the islands or online).

Tenerife holds an annual **Walking Festival** (May) with a week-long schedule of guided walks and cultural events (☏ 657 28 98 68, ⊕ tenerifewalkingfestival.com).

Climbing

Some of the best climbs are in **Las Cañadas** in the Parque Nacional del Teide – particularly around the rock pinnacles of Los Roques and La Catedrál. Check out **Tenerife Climbing House** (C/Asomadita 8 ☏ 689 88 68 09, ⊕ tenerifeclimbinghouse.com) for details.

Cycling

Tenerife and La Gomera are mountainous islands and many of the

Scuba diving centres

Costa Adeje Blue Bottom Diving, Avda España ☏ 922 71 41 85, ⊕ bluebottomdiving.co.uk.
Las Américas Excel Scuba Tenerife, Edificio El Dorado, Avda Santiago Puig 4 ☏ 664 16 56 36, ⊕ excel-scuba.com; Aqua Marina, Paseo Verode (behind *Hotel Oro Blanco*) ☏ 678 66 26 70, ⊕ aqua-marine.com.
Las Galletas Tenerife Scuba, C/Minerva 2, Costa del Silencio ☏ 922 78 55 84, ⊕ divingtenerifescuba.com; Dive Tenerife, C/Consuelo Alfonso Díaz Flores 12 ☏ 922 78 59 10, ⊕ divetenerife.com.
Los Gigantes Los Gigantes Diving Center, C/Poblado Marinero ☏ 922 86 04 31, ⊕ divingtenerife.co.uk.
Puerto de la Cruz Teide Divers, C/Corbeta, Edificio Los Organos ☏ 637 81 91 78, ⊕ teidedivers.com.
La Gomera Splash Gomera, Centro de Buceo, *Hotel Jardín Tecina*, Playa de Santiago ☏ 922 14 58 87, ⊕ splashgomera.es.

Bike rental

Playa de las Américas Bike4You, C/Galicia 24, Edificio Sunset ☎ 699 25 01 45, ⓦ bike4youtenerife.com; Bike Point Tenerife, Avda Quinta Centenario, Edificio las Terrazas ☎ 922 79 67 10, ⓦ bikepointtenerife.com.
Costa Adeje Avda Ernesto Sarti 3 ☎ 697 80 82 81, ⓦ cyclingtenerife.com.
Playa de Santiago, La Gomera, Gomera Cycling, Avda Marítima de Playa Santiago ☎ 922 89 51 45, ⓦ gomeracycling.com.
Valle Gran Rey Gomera Bikes, ⓦ gomera-bikes.com.

narrow roads are very busy, making neither ideal for leisurely cycling. They are, however, well suited to more exciting and challenging **day rides** and have become favourite winter training grounds for many professional cyclists, particularly given their ratio of height to surface area which makes for good **Tour de France** preparation.

Golf

The pleasant climate on the islands attracts **golf** enthusiasts year-round to Tenerife and La Gomera's **nine courses**, six of which are dotted around the resorts of southern Tenerife. The professional circuit usually includes at least one annual stop at Tenerife, most notably the **Tenerife Ladies' Open** held in May. For information on this and a detailed overview of the courses, visit the tourist board website ⓦ webtenerife.co.uk/tenerifegolf. **Green fees** are lower during summer months, when playing conditions are good with the trade winds keeping temperatures nicely cooled.

Golf courses

La Laguna Real Club de Golf de Tenerife (El Peñón, Tacoronte ☎ 922 63 66 07, ⓦ rcgt.es, Mon–Fri 8am–12.30pm).
Garachico and the Teno Buenavista Golf (C/Vista la Monje, Buenavista del Norte ☎ 922 12 90 34, ⓦ buenavistagolf.es, daily 8am–8pm).
The west coast Abama Golf (Playa San Juan ☎ 922 12 63 00 ⓦ abamagolf.com, daily 7am–8pm).
The southwest Resorts Golf Costa Adeje (Finca de los Olivos, Adeje ☎ 922 71 00 00, ⓦ golfcostaadeje.com, daily 7am–7pm); Golf las Américas (Avda Rafael Puig 10 ☎ 922 75 20 05, ⓦ golflasamericas.com, Mon–Fri 7am–7pm).
The southeast coast Amarilla Golf (San Miguel de Abona ⓦ amarillagolf.com, daily 8am–8.30pm); Golf del Sur (Avda Galván Bello, San Miguel de Abona ⓦ golfdelsur.es, daily 8.45am–7.30pm); Centro de Golf los Palos (nine hole; Ctra Guaza, Las Galletas, km7 ⓦ golflospalos.com, daily 8am–midnight).
Playa Santiago, La Gomera Tecina Golf (Lomada de Tecina, Playa de Santiago ☎ 922 14 59 50, ⓦ tecinagolf.com, daily 8am–7.30pm).

Directory A–Z

Addresses
Common **abbreviations** are: C/ for Calle (street); Ctra for Carretera (main road); Avda for Avenida (avenue); Edif for Edificio (a large block); and CC for Centro Commercial (a shopping centre or mall, often in an Edificio). An address given as C/Flores 24, 3° means third floor, 24 Flores Street.

Children
Children are warmly welcomed across Tenerife and La Gomera, where hotels and resorts cater extensively for families.

Complaints
All hotels, restaurants and other businesses have a **complaints book** (*hoja de reclamación*) in which complaints can be logged – and they are taken seriously.

Crime and emergencies
The **crime rate** in Tenerife is very low and it is considered one of the safest destinations in the world, but it is subject to petty crime, particularly in the purpose-built resorts, where pickpockets are known to operate. Theft from cars is also an issue at major cultural sights (such as Parque National del Teide) and you should never leave valuables unattended, even for a very short time. **Policia Nacional** are the local police; they have stations in all major towns and resorts. They should be your first port of call to report theft or any other crime. You'll find a list of stations, addresses and contact hours on their website ⓦpolicia.es. The **emergency number** is ☎112 for police, ambulance and fire brigade, and operators speak English, German and Spanish.

Customs
The Canary Islands are not part of the EU for customs purposes and are therefore to be treated the same as for **non-EU countries**. Current limits on what can be brought back to the UK are 18 litres of non-sparkling wine, 4 litres of spirits, 200 cigarettes and up to £390-worth of other goods and gifts. Check current limits at ⓦgov.uk.

Electricity
Standard 220-volt alternate current. Plugs have the standard, continental Europe two round prongs, so travellers from the UK will need an **adaptor**, while visitors from the US will also require a **voltage converter**.

Embassies and consulates
Britain, Plaza Weyler 8, Santa Cruz de Tenerife ☎928 26 25 08; **Ireland**, C/ Villalba Hervás 9-9°, Santa Cruz de Tenerife ☎922 24 56 71. The nearest **US** consulate is on Gran Canaria at Los Martínez de Escober 3, Oficina 7, Las Palmas de Gran Canaria ☎928 27 12 59.

Health
EU residents should present their **European Health Insurance Card** (or the new UK EHIC) to receive free treatment (from public clinics and hospitals only). Without an EHIC you will have to pay for any treatment received. A list of clinics and hospitals along with their contact details can be found at ⓦwebtenerife.co.uk. **Pharmacies** are indicated by a large green cross and are open Mon–Fri 9am–1pm and 4–8pm, Sat 9am–1pm. The nearest 24-hour emergency pharmacy is posted on every pharmacy door.

Internet

Wi-fi is now widely available in Tenerife and La Gomera, and many towns have hotspots. Disappointingly, some hotels still levy a charge for use of the wi-fi – though most do not. **Internet cafés** are still to be found in resorts on both islands.

Left luggage

There are no left luggage facilities at airports or ports on Tenerife and La Gomera. The best advice is to ask your accommodation if they can store luggage for you.

LGBTQ travellers

Tenerife is known as an LGBTQ-friendly destination and there's a well-established scene on the island, mainly around **Playa de las Américas** in the south and **Puerto de la Cruz** in the north. Current information and advice is available on ⓦholidayguru.ie and ⓦbringyourholidaysoutofthecloset.com.

Money and banks

The currency in the Canary Islands is the **euro** (€). For up-to-date conversion rates use ⓦxe.com. Bank branches and **ATMs** are plentiful in all main towns and resorts. Opening hours are Mon–Fri 9am–2pm, Sat 9am–1pm, except between late May and September, when banks close on Saturday, and during the Carnival period (February or March), when they close at midday. **Credit/debit card** purchases require you to show your passport or ID.

Opening hours

Shops in major towns and resorts are generally open Mon–Sat 10am–8pm and many places in resorts will open on Sundays too. In smaller towns and villages the **siesta** still operates, with shops closing 1.30–4.30pm.

Phones

Most hotels add surcharges to calls made from rooms, so it's cheaper to use a coin- or card-operated **payphone**. Various companies offer **phone cards** – available from newsagents, petrol stations and kiosks. Mobile phones work in the Canary Islands. **Roaming charges** for UK visitors vary following the UK's exit from the EU, check with your service provider before you travel.

Post offices

It usually takes four working days for a postcard or letter to reach the UK or mainland Europe (outside Spain). Post offices can be found in all the main towns and villages; take a ticket and wait for your number to come up.

Smoking

Smoking is not allowed in enclosed public spaces in the Canary Islands, but the sale of tobacco is not restricted.

Time

Both islands are in the same **time zone** as the UK and Ireland, five hours ahead of the US East Coast. Clocks go forward one hour in spring, back in autumn.

Tipping

In bars and taxis, rounding up to the next euro is fine. With waiters, a five- to ten-percent tip is perfectly adequate.

Tourist information

You'll find street maps and tourist information at **tourist offices** (*turismo*) across **Tenerife**, including at the airports. Most offices are open Mon–Fri 9am–5pm but some of the larger ones (Santa Cruz, Puerto de la Cruz, Reina Sofia Airport) also open on Saturdays and Sundays. Addresses and opening times can be found on

ⓦwebtenerife.co.uk. Tourist offices on **La Gomera** are located in San Sebastián, Valle Gran Rey and Playa de Santiago. Individual addresses and opening times can be found on ⓦlagomeratravel.

European **newspapers** reach Tenerife within a day of publication. The free, English-language newspaper produced on the island is *Tenerife News* (ⓦtenerifenews.com).

Travellers with disabilities

Access for travellers with disabilities varies greatly across the Canary Islands. Although most **hotels** now have adapted guest rooms and ramp access for wheelchair users, it's best to check before booking. Travellers to La Gomera will find fewer facilities. **Los Cristianos** is a particularly disability-friendly destination, with a barrier-free policy throughout the resort. Information on Canary Islands resorts, sites and hotel access for travellers with disabilities can be found at ⓦcanbedone.co.uk.

Festivals and events

Reyes Magos (Three Kings)

January 6
On the Eve of the Epiphany, the Three Kings arrive (sometimes riding camels) bearing gifts in ornate processions in major towns. This, rather than Dec 25, is traditionally the day for gift giving.

San Antonio Abad

January 17
Thousands of oxen, goats, horses and sundry pets take to the streets of Buenavista del Norte and La Matanza for their annual blessing.

Fiesta de San Sebastián (La Gomera)

January 20 ⓦsansebastiangomera.org
Singing and dancing to celebrate the town's patron saint.

Carnival

February/March
The biggest event of the year. Carnival festivities begin in Santa Cruz (see page 26), before moving on to other large towns, most notably Puerto de la Cruz.

Easter week (Semana Santa)

Late March/early April
ⓦsemanasantadelalaguna.com, ⓦcosta-adeje.es
Elaborate Easter processions take place on Good Friday in La Laguna, one a silent procession of religious brotherhoods. In Adeje, most of the town is involved in The Passion, a Biblical-sized, televised re-enactment of the crucifixion.

Fiesta de San Marcos, Agulo (La Gomera)

April 25 ⓦagulo.org
A statue of Agulo's patron saint, San Marcos, is surrounded by bonfires through which local young men run in a test of courage.

Romerías

May–Sept
Harvest festivals involving food, wine, carts pulled by oxen and townspeople in traditional costume known as Romerías take place across the islands throughout the summer. One of the largest and most spectacular is the Romería de San Roque, held in Garachico in August.

Carnival in Santa Cruz

Santa Cruz's **carnival** (🌐 carnavaldetenerife.com) is a wild week of mayhem and hedonism, attracting tens of thousands of people during Lent. Much of the action takes place in and around Plaza de España, where the streets fill with costume-clad locals dancing to live bands and DJs until dawn.

More for tourists than locals, the **Grand Procession** on Shrove Tuesday is a cavalcade of floats, bands, dancers and entertainers, who march and dance their way along the promenade. One of the highlights of carnival week is the **Burial of the Sardine** on Ash Wednesday, when a giant effigy of a sardine is paraded through the streets in a throng of wailing widows, most of them men, before being set alight amid fireworks. On **Carnival Friday**, just along the coast in Puerto de la Cruz, hundreds of cross-dressed men take to an obstacle course wearing comedy-sized, high-heeled shoes in what is rapidly becoming the most attended event of carnival - the **High Heels Marathon**. When Santa Cruz and Puerto de la Cruz wind down, carnival spreads out across the island.

Dia de la Cruz

May 3

Festival celebrating the founding of Tenerife's capital in which all the crosses are elaborately decorated in flowers. Celebrated by every place with "Cruz" in its name. In Los Realejos there's a three-hour fireworks display.

Día de Canarias

May 30

Public holiday marked by folk dances in the plazas of Santa Cruz and traditional towns. Shop assistants wear traditional costumes and the island's artisan produce is showcased in shops, markets and supermarkets.

Corpus Christi

May/June

On the Thursday that follows the eighth Sunday after Easter, Corpus Christi is celebrated. Major events are held in La Laguna and, a week later, in La Orotava – where streets are covered in floral carpets (see page 56).

Fiesta de San Juan

June 23 & 24

Midnight bathing and parties on Playa Jardín in Puerto de la Cruz on Midsummer's Eve, and herds of goats bathed in the harbour the next morning.

Fiesta Virgen del Carmen

July 16

The largest celebrations for the patron saint of fishermen and sailors are in Santa Cruz and Puerto de la Cruz on Tenerife, and in Valle Gran Rey and

Public holidays

January 1 New Year's Day
January 6 Feast of the Epiphany
February 2 Purification of the Virgin of Candelaria
Carnival Tuesday (Feb/March)
Good Friday (March/Apr)
May 1 May Day
May 30 Día de Canarias
August 15 Ascension Day
October 12 Spain Day
November 2 All Saints Day
December 8 Feast of the Immaculate Conception
December 25 Christmas Day

Playa de Santiago on La Gomera. They include the Virgin being taken out to sea amid a flotilla of boats.

Fiesta Virgen de la Candelaria

August 15
Thousands of pilgrims walk across the island to celebrate the Virgen de Candelaria's patron day, and watch an elaborate re-enactment of her discovery.

Fiesta de Cristobal Colón

September 6
Anniversary of the departure of Columbus (Colón) from San Sebastián on his first voyage to the Americas.

Fiesta de la Virgen del Socorro

September 7 ⓦ el-socorro.com
Güímar puts on a large procession from the church to the sea in honour of the town's patron saint.

San Andrés

November 29 ⓦ tablasdesanandres. net
Wine festival in Icod de los Vinos and Puerto de la Cruz to celebrate the grape harvest. In Icod, youths careen down near-vertical streets on greased trays.

Chronology

20 million years ago The island of La Gomera is formed.

6 million years ago The island of Tenerife begins to take on its present shape.

900–400BC Berber (Amazigh) groups settle on the islands.

c.300BC The earliest known mentions of the Canary Islands are made by Plato (428–348 BC), in his references to Atlantis.

40BC The first written account of a landing in the Canary Islands is made by a fleet serving King Juba II, the Roman client king of Mauritania.

c.140 Ptolemy (c.100–160) draws his world map, on which the Canary Islands form the edge of the known world.

1392 Two Guanche shepherds find a statue of the Virgin Mary on a beach in Güímar.

1404 French adventurer Baron Jean de Béthencort steps ashore in Lanzarote, beginning the process of the conquest of the Canary Islands.

1488 An island-wide rebellion begins in La Gomera, costing the governor's life.

1492 Christopher Columbus stops over in La Gomera en route to the New World.

1493–96 Tenerife is conquered by Spanish conquistador Alonso Fernández de Lugo.

1550–1670 The production of wine takes the place of sugar cane farming to become Tenerife's predominant industry.

1706 The port of Garachico is destroyed by a volcanic eruption.

1797 Admiral Nelson attempts to take Santa Cruz and loses his right arm in the process.

1817 La Laguna university is founded.

1822 Santa Cruz takes over from La Laguna as the island's capital.

1852 Santa Cruz becomes a free port.

1880 Banana cultivation is introduced to Tenerife and La Gomera.

1880s Tenerife enjoys increasing popularity as a tourist destination among the European gentry.

1909 The most recent volcanic eruption occurs on Tenerife.

1927 Tenerife becomes seat of government for the Western Canary Islands; Gran Canaria governs the Eastern Canary Islands.

1936 Franco launches his coup from Tenerife, sparking the Spanish Civil War.

1959 The first charter flights to Tenerife herald a new era of tourism.

1982 The Canaries become an autonomous region within Spain.

1986 The Canary Islands join the EU, though they remain outside the customs union.

1999 San Cristóbal de La laguna joins La Gomera's Garajonay and Tenerife's Parque Nacional del Teide as recognised Unesco World Heritage sites.

2007 La Orotava goes into the Guinness Book of Records for creation of the world's largest sand carpet.

2009 El Silbo Gomero declared Intangible Cultural Heritage by Unesco.

2012 Physicists set a new record of 143km for quantum teleportation, transmitting photons between observatories on La Palma and Tenerife.

2015 Anaga Massif recognised by Unesco as a Biosphere Reserve.

Spanish

Once you get into it, **Spanish** is one of the easiest languages around, and in Tenerife and la Gomera you'll be helped everywhere by people who are eager to try to understand even the most faltering attempt. English is spoken in the main tourist areas, but you'll get a far better reception if you try communicating with *canarios* in their own tongue.

For non-native speakers, the easiest difference to notice in the **pronunciation** of Canarian Spanish is the absence of a "lisp" on the letter "c" before vowels – which is replaced by an "s" sound. Thus Barcelona, pronounced Barthelona in Spain, becomes Barselona. However, in its most casual form, the

Canarian pronunciation doesn't even really bother with "s" sounds at all, particularly where these come at the end of a word – so gracias becomes gracia; and buenos días, bueno día.

For more than a brief introduction to the language, pick up a copy of the **Rough Guide Spanish Phrasebook**.

Pronunciation
The rules of **pronunciation** are pretty straightforward and are strictly observed.

A somewhere between the A sound of back and that of father.

E as in get.

I as in police.

O as in hot.

U as in rule.

C is spoken like an S before E and I, hard otherwise: *cerca* is pronounced "sairka" (standard Spanish would pronounce it "thairka").

G is a guttural H sound (like the ch in loch) before E or I, a hard G elsewhere – *gigante* becomes "higante".

H is always silent.

J is the same as a guttural G: *jamón* is "hamon".

LL sounds like an English Y: *tortilla* is pronounced "torteeya".

N is as in English unless it has a tilde (accent) over it, when it becomes NY: *mañana* sounds like "manyana".

QU is pronounced like an English K.

R is rolled, RR doubly so.

V sounds more like B, *vino* becoming "beano".

X has an S sound before consonants, normal X before vowels.

Z is spoken like an S, so *cerveza* becomes "sairbaisa" (standard Spanish would pronounce it "thairbaitha").

Words and phrases

Basics

Yes, No, OK Sí, No, Vale
Please, Thank you Por favor, Gracias
Where?, When? ¿Dónde?, ¿Cuándo?
What?, How much? ¿Qué?, ¿Cuánto?
Here, There Aquí, Allí
This, That Esto, Eso
Now, Later Ahora, Más tarde
Open, Closed Abierto/a, Cerrado/a
With, Without Con, Sin
Good, Bad Buen(o)/a, Mal(o)/a
Big, Small Gran(de), Pequeño/a
Cheap, Expensive Barato, Caro
Hot, Cold Caliente, Frío
More, Less Más, Menos
Today, Tomorrow Hoy, Mañana
Yesterday Ayer
The bill La cuenta

Greetings and responses

Hello, Goodbye Hola, Adiós
Good morning Buenos días
Good afternoon/night Buenas tardes/noches
See you later Hasta luego
Sorry Lo siento/Disculpe

Excuse me Con permiso/Perdón
How are you? ¿Cómo está (usted)?
I (don't) understand (No) Entiendo
You're welcome/not at all De nada
Do you speak English? ¿Habla (usted) inglés?
I (don't) speak Spanish (No) Hablo español
My name is. . . Me llamo. . .
What's your name? ¿Como se llama usted?
I am English / Soy inglés(a) /
** Scottish /** escocés(a) /
** Welsh /** galés(a) /
** Australian /** australiano(a) /
** Canadian** canadiense /
** American** americano(a) /
** Irish** irlandés(a) /
** New Zealander** Nueva Zelandés(a)

Hotels, transport and directions

I want Quiero
I'd like Quisiera
Do you know. . .? ¿Sabe . . .?
I don't know No sé
There is (is there)? (¿)Hay(?)
Give me (one like that) Deme (uno así)
Do you have...? ¿Tiene......?
... the time ... la hora
... a room ... una habitación
... with two beds/ with a double bed ..... con dos camas/con cama matrimonial
... with shower/ bath ... con ducha/baño
It's for one person Es para una persona
For one night para una noche
For one week para una semana
How do I get to.....? ¿Por donde se va a...?
Left, right, straight on Izquierda, derecha, todo recto
Where is.....? ¿Dónde está...?
... the bus station . . . la estación de guaguas
... the nearest bank . . . el banco mas cercano
... the post office . . . el correos/la oficina de correos
... the toilet . . . el baño/los aseos
Where does the bus to . . . leave from? ¿De dónde sale la guagua para...?
I'd like a (return) ticket to . . . Quisiera un billete (de ida y vuelta) para...
What time does it leave? ¿A qué hora sale?

Numbers and days

1 un/uno/una
2 dos
3 tres
4 cuatro
5 cinco
6 seis
7 siete
8 ocho
9 nueve
10 diez
11 once
12 doce
13 trece
14 catorce
15 quince
16 diez y seis
17 diez y siete
18 diez y ocho
19 diez y nueve
20 veinte
21 veintiuno
30 treinta
40 cuarenta
50 cincuenta
60 sesenta
70 setenta
80 ochenta
90 noventa
100 cien(to)
101 ciento uno
200 doscientos
500 quinientos
1000 mil
Monday lunes
Tuesday martes
Wednesday miércoles
Thursday jueves
Friday viernes
Saturday sábado
Sunday domingo
today hoy
yesterday ayer
tomorrow mañana

Food and drink

aceitunas olives
agua water
ahumados smoked fish
al ajillo with olive oil and garlic

a la marinera seafood cooked with garlic, onions and white wine
a la parilla charcoal-grilled
a la plancha grilled on a hot plate
a la romana fried in batter
albóndigas meatballs
almejas clams
anchoas anchovies
arroz rice
asado roast
bacalao cod
berenjena aubergine/eggplant
bocadillo bread roll sandwich
boquerones small, anchovy-like fish, usually served in vinegar
café (con leche) (white) coffee
calamares squid
cangrejo crab
cebolla onion
cerveza beer
champiñones mushrooms
chorizo spicy sausage
croquetas croquettes, usually with bits of ham inside
cuchara spoon
cuchillo knife
empanada slices of fish/meat pie
ensalada salad
ensaladilla russian salad (diced vegetables in mayonnaise, often with tuna)
fresa strawberry
gambas prawns
gofio finely ground mix of wheat, barley or maize, usually accompanying soups and stews
hígado liver
huevos eggs
jamón serrano cured ham
jamón de york regular ham
langostinos langoustines
lechuga lettuce
manzana apple
mejillones mussels
mojo garlic dressing available in "rojo" (spicy "red" version) and "verde" ("green", made with coriander)
naranja orange
ostras oysters
pan bread
papas arrugadas unpeeled new potatoes, boiled dry in salted water

papas alioli potatoes in garlic mayonnaise

papas bravas fried potatoes in a spicy tomato sauce

pimientos peppers

pimientos de padrón small peppers, with the odd hot one

piña pineapple

pisto assortment of cooked vegetables, similar to ratatouille

plátano banana

pollo chicken

puchero traditional Canarian stew of meat and vegetables

pulpo octopus

queso cheese

rancho canario traditional Canarian chickpea, noodle and meat soup

salchicha sausage

setas oyster mushrooms

sopa soup

té tea

tenedor fork

tomate tomato

tortilla española potato omelette

tortilla francesa plain omelette

vino (blanco, rosado, tinto) (white, rosé, red) wine

zarzuela Canarian fish stew

zumo juice

Glossary

avenida avenue

barranco gorge/ravine

barrio suburb or neighbourhood

calle street or road

centro commercial shopping and entertainment mall

chiringuito beach bar

edificio building

ermita hermitage/chapel

hacienda large manor house

guagua local name for buses

Guanche aboriginal inhabitants of the Canary Islands

iglesia church

menú del día daily menu in a restaurant

mercado market

mirador view point

Mudéjar Spanish-Moorish architecture

parador state-run hotel, usually housed in buildings of historic interest

playa beach

plaza square

terraza terracem, veranda or temporary summer outdoor bar/club

SMALL PRINT

Publishing Information
Second edition 2022

Distribution
UK, Ireland and Europe
Apa Publications (UK) Ltd; sales@roughguides.com
United States and Canada
Ingram Publisher Services; ips@ingramcontent.com
Australia and New Zealand
Booktopia; retailer@booktopia.com.au
Worldwide
Apa Publications (UK) Ltd; sales@roughguides.com
Special Sales, Content Licensing and CoPublishing
Rough Guides can be purchased in bulk quantities at discounted prices. We can
create special editions, personalised jackets and corporate imprints tailored to
your needs. sales@roughguides.com.
roughguides.com

A catalogue record for this book is available from the British Library
The publishers and authors have done their best to ensure the accuracy
and currency of all the information in **Pocket Rough Guide Tenerife & La
Gomera**, however, they can accept no responsibility for any loss, injury, or
inconvenience sustained by any traveller as a result of information or advice
contained in the guide.

Rough Guide Credits
Editors: Mundy Walsh, Kate Drynan,
Joanna Reeves
Cartography: Carte
Picture editor: Piotr Kala
Layout: Greg Madejak

Original design: Richard Czapnik
Head of DTP and Pre-Press:
Katie Bennett
Head of Publishing: Kate Drynan

Help us update

We've gone to a lot of effort to ensure that this edition of the **Pocket Rough Guide Tenerife & La Gomera** is accurate and up-to-date. However, things change – places get "discovered", opening hours are notoriously fickle, restaurants and rooms raise prices or lower standards. If you feel we've got it wrong or left something out, we'd like to know, and if you can remember the address, the price, the hours, the phone number, so much the better.

Please send your comments with the subject line "**Pocket Rough Guide Tenerife & La Gomera Update**" to mail@uk.roughguides.com. We'll credit all contributions and send a copy of the next edition (or any other Rough Guide if you prefer) for the very best emails.

SMALL PRINT

Photo Credits

(Key: T-top; C-centre; B-bottom; L-left; R-right)

Index

148

NOTES